Hope to See You Soon

Revital Shiri-Horowitz

Wilmette Public Library
1242 Wilmette Avenue
Wilmette, Il 60091
847-256-5025

ISBN: 978-1-63443-050-0

Translated by Shira Atik

Editing: Nance Morris Adler

Designer: Vered Mizrahi

edicated to Amnon,

my partner and best friend,

with love

Summer 2005

I'm sitting on my front porch, staring down at the street. Very few cars pass through my quiet street, day or night. During the day, there's an affable commotion: people coming and going, cars pulling in and out, children laughing, neighbors chatting across the porches, the squeak of the clothesline, the sounds of doors slamming and children running downstairs, then back upstairs for dinner, the sound of doors locking. Then an unsettling quiet sets in. During the late-night hours, the streets are almost completely noiseless. From time to time a distant siren or a barking dog punctures the silence, but never anything more than that.

I spend my days and nights watching the world outside, a world in which I play no part at all. I don't even make a cameo appearance. I've been here for a few months now, living in this lovely, relatively inexpensive little apartment in the heart of Tel Aviv. My grandparents, who originally owned the apartment, had rented it out for many years. When I came to Israel, alone, I moved in. My siblings' share of the rental money goes straight into their bank accounts.

I had always dreamed of living in the bustling center of Tel Aviv. I was sure that if I did, my own existence would fuse with the city's busy, cosmopolitan life that I thirsted for. I thirsted for the sounds, the language, the reading of the morning papers, the visits to the local green-grocer, the theater, maybe a subscription to the symphony. I painstakingly plotted out how I would get here, how I would live in this apartment in which I had spent so much of my childhood. I yearned for the moment when I would wake up in the big city, go out on the streets, speak the local language - my mother-tongue. How I would savor every taste, every delight, of this city. But instead, I imprisoned myself in my apartment. There is no place for me in the world outside my window.

I fill my days and nights with my own affairs. I spy on other people's lives and fill up my own life by telling myself their stories. I know my neighbors well, not necessarily because we're friends but because I watch them and listen in on them whenever I can. I know how they spend their days, how they live their lives. Sometimes I am beleaguered by worry, and I can't calm down until I am certain that all my neighbors have returned home safely. If one of them is late, I patrol the street until I see his or her car approaching; only then can I calm down and return to my routine. Although they are always cordial when they see me, my neighbors don't know the first thing about me. To them, I am merely the lonely tenant who moved to the third floor, to Apartment 11, a few months ago. And really, why should they be interested in someone who rarely leaves her house, who barely even opens the door or engages in conversation? Maybe they wonder why I never go out, or why I never talk to them. Not that they've ever tried to talk to me, either, beyond a perfunctory greeting in the hallway. I'm not offended by their lack of interest; after all, they have a lot going on, and I play no part in their lives.

I can tell from their body language how stressed they are; I can tell from their behavior how compassionate they are, how much they love their fellow human beings, how kind they are to animals. I study their habits and fill in the missing pieces. I embroider a history for each of them: a childhood, adolescence, sometimes a marriage. Their life stories are always intriguing, filled with dramas large and small, with loves and hatreds, with joys and sorrows, and in each of their lives I play a vital role, creating, controlling, and shaping everything that happens. I am the one who determines their actions.

Real life takes place not just in the outside world, but in my memory as well. The world that I choose- my own world- is rich and intriguing, and I control its flow and rhythm. That's all I need. I've had enough of the outside world to last me a lifetime. I find that I am able to fill my world with books that I borrow from the local library, to burrow into myself. My imagination fills my days and my nights, and I don't need anything else.

I look outside- here comes Roni. Thirty years old, approximately, and always meticulously dressed. He is married to Daphna, and they have a seven-month old daughter, Na'ama. I remember when they brought her home; she was so tiny and sweet. I couldn't restrain myself, and I asked if I could touch her small, soft hand. The little one's hair was so black and thick and long, not really suited for someone so tiny. Daphna looked tired. After we spoke, Roni and Daphna, retreated into their apartment- first floor, on the right- as fast as they could. I know their names from the mailboxes, and their life story, which nobody ever told me, includes love and longing and even an affair (It was Daphna who was cheating on Roni, not the other way around. He's too dependent on his wife, too attuned to her).

Roni's always in a hurry, and there is a perpetual look of worry on his face. The wrinkle between his brows deepens when he leaves the house in the morning, and when he comes home, usually at around seven, his face looks tired and his movements are

7

sluggish. He has a particular routine for parking his car: first he turns off the engine, then he opens the driver-side door and puts one foot on the ground while he gathers up his briefcase and all his scattered papers. Then he slowly gets out of the car and absent-mindedly walks into the building. Once or twice I've seen him accidentally slam the car door on his foot, bite his lip in pain, and continue on his way. I never really stopped to talk to him, to ask him what he does, but in my mind he is an accountant, and numbers are constantly floating around in his head, day and night. Na'ama is the only one who can bring a smile to his face; when that happens, the groove between his eyes disappears, if only for a moment.

My heart goes out to him. When I see him, I think of Yonatan, and I wonder if he'll grow up to be that serious, that absorbed in his own world. Will he choose to study computers, or will he follow his childhood dream of becoming an actor? Perhaps he'll decide to see the world, to travel, to eke out a living, to live as frugally as possible so he can afford to travel the world? Sweet Yonatan. What time is it where he is? It's early morning; is he already on his way to school? I come inside and wander anxiously around the apartment. Then I crawl between the sheets and try, unsuccessfully, to fall asleep.

A few hours later, I go back out to the porch. It's nine in the evening, and Dahlia is putting Rotem to bed. I hear her telling him to brush his teeth, I imagine his little mouth twisting in protest, I hear his plaintive voice: "Three more minutes, Mommy, just three more minutes." I smile to yself; it's always three minutes, never two, never four, only three. Does he even understand the concept of time? I remember Abigail when she was that age, pleading to

8

stay up later, promising to get up early, a promise she never could keep. I turn my attention back to the voices, and I look outside. It's time for Iris to come home. She's about seventeen now, and she lives one floor above me. I've been watching her since I got here, and she knows it. She looks up at the porch, searching for my gaze, nodding her head in greeting when she comes in or goes out, fully aware that I am following her movements. On Mondays she wears gym clothes. Most days she leaves the house full of energy, but today she's walking more slowly than usual. Has something bad happened to her? I'll never find out, I'll never know, but in my imagination, she's smarting from an unrequited love. I know she'll have other disappointments, that are how life is, but for now, she can't conceive of the hardships that await her. She doesn't understand. Perhaps it's better that way.

July 23, 1980

Dear Michal,

I can't believe I'm here. When my mother told me that we were going to visit her aunt in Eilat- in July!- I almost fainted. This is so, so not how I wanted to spend my summer. Instead of splashing around with you on the amazing Acadia Beach in Herziliya, I'm stuck here in Eilat, getting scorched, dying of boredom, and waiting for what my mother calls our "family bonding experience" to finally end.

My older sister's getting on my nerves with all her self-righteousness, whispering with my mother all day long. I'm running out of patience. If only you were here with me. Yesterday I found myself thinking about how we first met, and it made me laugh, remembering how your father, who always called me "latke," had come with you to register you for high school, and I was there with my mother, and he seemed so nice, and so did you. I wanted to be your friend, but I didn't know how to tell you. They didn't even put us in the same class, but luckily we spent that week of pre-army training together in that garbage dump Bet Lid, and you ended up sleeping in the bed right next to mine, and we started talking, and we haven't stopped.

I want you to know that you're my best friend and I miss you so much. Even though I met this very cute boy here, I'd still rather spend time with you (OK, it's true, he hardly noticed me). I have two more weeks here. Hope you're having a blast and that Tomer has finally figured out how amazing you are, and that you're not just a good student who helps him with his homework.

That's it for now. Hang in there, and write soon.

Missing you tons,

Tamari

July 31, 1980

Dear Tamari,

I was ready to give up on you, since you promised me that you'd write as soon as you got there and I had to wait two whole weeks for a letter. I would go downstairs ten times a day to check the mailbox, and my mom would laugh at me and tell me that you're only going to be gone for a month, not a year.

Well, whatever. The important thing is that you wrote me. The minute I saw your handwriting on the envelope I ran into my room and kicked my brother out. He was furious. He couldn't understand why he had to leave his own bedroom just because of a little piece of paper full of nonsense. Sometimes I wish there were no such things as little brothers.

It's not so much fun here without you. We've been spending our weekends at the beach, the whole family, and that's been nice, but other than that it's really boring here. I've had enough of this vacation. That pesky Rina calls me almost every day, as if the fact that you're not here means she can be my substitute best friend, but don't worry, she doesn't stand a chance.

I go to the library at least three times a week. The librarian says that if I read all the books in alphabetical order, by the end of the summer I'll have gone through the entire collection. She's nice, the librarian. I offered to help her write people's names on the cards when they borrow books, and once in a while, when she's there by herself, she really does need help., She must get bored when there's nobody there. I also help her put the books back on the shelves. I'm not interested in Tomer anymore.

I met this amazing boy in the library, Shachar. I think he likes me, too, because all of a sudden he's coming to the library all the time. Even the librarian noticed.

That's about it. It must be very hot where you are, and I bet you're very tan. I'm counting the days until you come home.

Your loyal friend forever,

Michal

φφφ

Tamari had no idea what she was missing. I was disappointed when she didn't want to come with me to the "Gesher" seminar on beautiful Mount Canaan. No matter how much I tried to convince her, she refused. To my surprise, that seminar turned out to be a spiritual experience for me. Everything that happened was new. People were asking all kinds of big, existential questions, and I suddenly felt like all these new and fascinating worlds that I had never encountered were opening up right before my eyes. I shared a room with four other girls; I was the only one who wasn't Orthodox, and they went out of their way to make sure I felt comfortable. The differences between our day-to-day lives were enormous. They blessed everything. "Blessed be God" for this, "Thank God" for that. Every single thing they ate had to be blessed. We even have to recite a long blessing after every meal. It takes forever. All these things were new to me, and I was mesmerized.

One of the girls I met at the seminar told me her strategy: as long as she doesn't eat bread, she doesn't have to say the full blessing after the meal, so whenever she can, she skips the bread. Who knew that being Orthodox could be good for your figure? On one of the mornings, they divided us up into three groups. Everyone had to choose which word described them best: Jew, Israeli, or human being. I thought about it for a long time before I decided that first and foremost I'm an Israeli. That ended up being the smallest group. Most of the religious people said they were primarily Jewish, most of the secular people said they were primarily humans, and I waffled between "Israeli" and "human,"

13

until I decided that I am, above all, Israeli. Why? No real reason. It just felt right. I'm an Israeli through and through.

Right before Shabbat there was a real sense of celebration. At home, we scarf down our dinner on Friday nights so we can get to the parties, but at Seminar, the atmosphere was different: there weren't any parties, so there was no reason to rush. I wondered what Shabbat looked like through religious eyes. The religious people on Seminar were very serious. They cared about who you were as a human being, and if anybody needed help, they were the first to volunteer. All these different worlds were coming together, and I found it fascinating, meeting all these people who were so different from me. I even got a crush on one of the counselors. I heard through the grapevine that he was studying in a yeshiva and that he was engaged, and I prayed that the part about his engagement was wrong. The other part of the rumor didn't bother me nearly as much.

Shabbat there was like nothing I'd ever experienced before. The atmosphere was very special. It wasn't just another day, it was Shabbat, the day of the Sabbath Queen, and for me, who was celebrating it for the first time, it was a truly extraordinary experience. There was a sense of elevation, something almost mystical that was sweeping me up, and I wanted to know as much as I could about God, and prayers, and blessings, and all of a sudden, my usual life seemed so dull. When Shabbat was almost over, and just before we could see three stars in the sky, we started hiking towards Tsfat. On the way, I saw one of the most beautiful sunsets I'd ever seen. The sun blazed all different shades of violet, and it looked as if it had been split across the middle by a cloud. I stood there for a long time, entranced, until the sun finally sunk out of sight.

During the seminar I met Aviva, who is one year older than me. We spent a lot of time together, talking non-stop. I wanted to get to know her better, to learn more about her. She told me about her day-to-day life, and I told her about mine. Among other things, I told her about Tamari, and she said she'd love to meet her and maybe the two of us could spend a Shabbat with her. Her kindness really won me over.

She said that after high school she was going to marry her fiancé, who was studying in a yeshiva. I told her I couldn't understand how she could know now that in two more years she'd still want to marry this guy, and how could she be so sure, at such a young age, that she wanted to spend her whole life with just one person. She told me she knew it with absolute certainty, and that she's known him since she was little and she has no doubt that they would be happy together. At that point, my plans included school, travel, and army service. A wedding was the last thing on my mind.

ϕϕϕ

Tamari wasn't exactly thrilled when I told her about my experiences on Seminar. In fact, she was somewhat horrified by the intensity of my experience, and she was afraid I was going to turn my whole life upside-down and become religious. In her mind, being exposed to something different was dangerous; that was her excuse for not coming with me. She was sure I'd been brainwashed, and she couldn't understand "my new outlook on the world." She begged me not to buy into the idea that life with the "Dosim" -religious people- was calmer and better, and tried to convince me that this was just another example of the grass being greener on the other side of the fence. I was only seeing part of the picture, she said, and that there were bad things, too, about the way they lived. Things I wouldn't like at all.

She was so troubled by my enthusiasm that she presented me with a terrifying scenario: I'd become religious, live in Jerusalem, marry at the age of seventeen, have an army of children, and constantly say things like "With God's help" and "Thank God." She urged me to forget about this "fantasy week," as she called it, and go back to our "normal" life. I didn't really understand why she was so scared. Just because I was excited by what I saw and learned didn't mean I was going to become religious; it just gave me a window into another kind of life that I knew nothing about, even though there are probably people right down the street who live that way. Yes, I had found the experience captivating, but the only thing I wanted was to learn more about this world that was so different from mine, to understand things more. Becoming religious wasn't on my agenda. I enjoyed- and still enjoy- wearing pants and sunbathing on the beach in my swimsuit. I don't mind wearing a skirt once in a while, like when I go to a party on Friday night, but I wouldn't want to wear one all the time. I had never even considered changing my lifestyle. And the truth is, there were things I had seen that I didn't like. It irked me that boys and girls couldn't sit together in synagogue, and that only boys could be called up to the Torah. (Many years later, I was able to bypass this inequality when I visited egalitarian synagogues, where I felt more comfortable, and closer to Judaism.)

While I was on "Gesher," Tamari bumped into Chagai, the neighbors' son, whom she'd had a crush on in elementary school. She used to follow him around like a puppy-dog, and he never even noticed. His family had just come back from a year in the United States, where his parents had been shlichim- Israeli emissaries who travel all around the world to teach people about Israeli culture. He was planning to start high school with us. She was so enamored with his appearance, especially his height and his muscular arms, and- of course- his tan. When she saw him, she couldn't even speak. She did just about every trick she could think of, some of which were ridiculous, to get his attention. But as it turned out, she didn't have to try so hard, because it was immediately clear that he was smitten with her. She was pretty, and her uncontainable vitality was infectious; it was hard not to fall in love with her. She dumped her previous boyfriend with dizzying speed, and it took him- well, it took his ego- a long time to recover from the blow. But Chagai had always been the object of her desire, and when she found out that he had returned, nothing could stop her from trying to get him for herself. When she found out that I had no plans to become religious, she calmed down, but the fact that I had a crush on a "dosi" boy named

Simcha cracked her up. She dismissed the "signs of mutual love" that I claimed existed between us, and that made me sad, maybe because I thought she was right. Deep down I was still hoping that he felt something special towards me.

It goes without saying that she didn't consider me her rival when it came to capturing Chagai's heart. After all, I was much less pretty than she was, and shyer. And the truth is, I wasn't interested in him.

When I got back from "Gesher", she told me that her mother had started working as a secretary at a garage in, so if I went to her house after school, we'd have some time to ourselves. Tamari's mother changed jobs as often as a pig farmer changes his socks. She couldn't hold on to any job, and whenever something went wrong, she blamed the rest of the world.

26 Kislev 5741, Blessed be God

December 4, 1980

Dear Tamari,

Here I am writing to you, just like I promised. I'm glad I decided to spend Chanukah at Aviva's house in Jerusalem. I'm taking advantage of our host's afternoon siesta, when everything is quiet and I can concentrate. Before you start writing me panicky letters, let me reassure you: I haven't turned religious. Not even close.

Jerusalem is cold in the winter, and at night you can hear the wind whistling. I had trouble falling asleep last night because of the jackals, and no matter how hard I tried to cover my ears, nothing helped. I even put a pillow over my head, but I could still hear the jackals howling and howling. I was sure that any minute they'd burst into Aviva's room and devour both of us. I woke up this morning with a terrible headache. I hope I can sleep tonight, even if the jackals howl. I'm so wiped out....

My hosts are very nice. Aviva has two married brothers and a sister who's six years younger than her. Her nieces and nephews are always running around the house, because Aviva's mother watches them when their parents are at work. Things are hectic here, but in a good way, and people show each other a lot of love and consideration, which amazes me. In my house, everything's completely chaotic, and the kids are always fighting, but in their house, there's a kind of peacefulness. Aviva doesn't complain about her sister, even though in my opinion she's a real pain in the neck. In fact, Aviva is very nice to her, and she puts up with all her nonsense.

Celebrating Chanukah in Jerusalem is an awesome experience. It's too bad you're not here to see all the lights twinkling on top of the city's ancient buildings. Every night, Aviva takes me to celebrate Chanukah with a different family. I ate so many latkes and jelly donuts, I must have put on ten pounds in the last three days. She also took me to their synagogue. It's an ancient building, very small, not far from their house. It's always full, and everyone there seems to know everyone else. It feels welcoming and warm. I think that if you're Orthodox, you're never alone. In the three days that I've been here, Aviva's mother hosted one family that just had a baby, and another family- their "adopted family"- that came here from America a few months ago. She knits sweaters for her children, her grandchildren, her neighbors, and I don't know who else. The door is always open, and the neighbors come and go all day long, except for right after lunch, when they close the door and everyone goes home for their afternoon nap.

Aviva introduced me to her fiancé, a sweet guy, kind of serious, but of course that's exactly what I expected. On Friday night we're going to his yeshiva for the Shabbat service; I hear it's usually packed. Should be interesting. In the meantime, Aviva has taken me to the Old City and the Western Wall where I wrote my prayers on a small piece of paper and stuck it in the cracks between the stones. Then we walked to Yemin Moshe, which is right near Aviva's house. Tomorrow morning we're planning to go to the Knesset. Who knows, maybe we'll even go on a tour.

Life here feels pleasant and safe. People sincerely care about each other, and they're always willing to help. The whole business of prayer, and God this and God that, still feels strange to me, but I could get used to this if I wanted to (not that I want to right now).

See you in four days!

Kisses,

Michal

2005

Last week, Dan sent me some photos of Yonatan and Abigail. He enclosed a hand-written note, saying he hoped that now that I have photos of our kids, I might want to meet them and see for myself how awesome they are. It's been months since I last saw my children, or heard their voices. I wasn't there for them in times of joy or in times of sorrow. They must be angry and confused; maybe one day they'll understand. Maybe one day I'll be able to explain it to them, face to face, but that day hasn't come yet. I put the photos on my television stand, across from my bed. Yonatan looks so grown-up and serious- not too serious, I hope. There's no reason for him to carry the burden of the world on his narrow, sloping shoulders; they couldn't handle it, anyway. Yonatan's brown eyes are searching for love. He's looking at the camera as if he's asking, "Now what?" He's wearing an orange shirt, and the blue background behind him highlights the delicate features of his face. His eyes look out at me softly, and I can't stop looking back at them.

In the other picture, Yonatan and Abigail are standing next to each other, smiling tentatively at the camera. Abigail seems a little lost. She's looking at the camera with an expression of impatience or insecurity, or maybe both. She looks so much like Dan; it's only at the corners of her mouth that I can detect any resemblance to my mother, of blessed memory. She's standing next to Yonatan, her arms at her sides, wearing a white button-down blouse tucked into a black knee-length skirt. I say her name, trying to soothe myself. Abigail, the name of King David's wife. Abi- father; Gail- joy. Abby, that's what everyone calls her; Abby, my sweet girl. And there I am, standing in my bedroom, muttering Abigail's name and staring directly into Yonatan's eyes until I finally collapse on the bed, stick my head between my pillows, and scream with all my might, a long wail of pain that is absorbed by the bedding. Then I flip over onto my back and lie awake all night, until the sun rises and redeems me.

In his letter, Dan writes that Yonatan is going into eleventh grade. Abby is finishing up seventh grade and she needs her mother. He needs me, too, Dan writes. Enough with the anger and the grudges, it's time to start a new chapter. "Come home," he writes. I throw the letter into the trash, then immediately take the can down to the building's garbage room so I won't be tempted to read it again: his words, his lies, his ruses. I'm fed up with him and his pleas. I no longer believe a word he says; I haven't believed him for years, not since before I did what I did and left him and our children.

As I said, I put the photos of the kids in my bedroom. I had two days of misery and tears, but now I'm done crying. I don't feel my pain, or theirs, anymore. They stand across from me, morning and night, staring at me, but I vigilantly stick to my routine. I fill my time by keeping track of my neighbors. Fortunately, there's a nice sum of money in my bank account, an inheritance from my parents; that allows me to live tolerably well; anyway, I need very little. Roni and Na'ama went to the playground behind our building. I watch them from the laundry room, and notice that Na'ama's hair is tied back in a braid. Roni is pushing her on the swing and singing to her; Na'ama joins in. I can hear the sounds of the melodies. How wonderful that the municipal playground is so close.

23

I smile to myself and hum quietly: swing up, swing down, swing all around, who do I see, just you and me.

December 29, 1980

Hey Michali,

In three days we're starting a new year- a new decade, actually- and you're in Jerusalem. It's too bad for both of us, really, because Tali's throwing a huge party and you're going to miss it. All the coolest kids in the class are going, and so are the youth movement kids. Tali's mom is loading up the house with food and drinks- she hasn't realized that we'll be taking care of our own drinks.... I bet the party will last all night, and if everything goes well, my first kiss of the New Year will be with Chagai (who still hasn't noticed that I exist). Anyway, I'm putting this letter right into your mailbox so it'll be waiting for you as soon as you get home.

You write that you like it there, that you're going on trips and doing all kinds of fun things, and I'm a little jealous because I had a pretty crappy week. Like I wrote, Chagai doesn't really notice my existence, at least not as a woman, and I've come to the conclusion that I'm like a sister to him. That's not what I had in mind! Maybe I'll have to do something extreme, like kiss him on New Year's Eve. After all, we're feminists, right? Or maybe I should wave my bra in front of his eyes so he can see that I'm more than just a good basketball player. We'll have to wait and see, but I have a feeling it's going to be a very interesting evening.

I hope you've been doing some of the homework at your friend's house, because I don't think the last day before school will be enough time to finish all the work we got over "vacation." I don't understand why they even bother to call it vacation, if all we're doing is homework. In any case, I've decided that this year I'm

25

going to "take my future in hand," as my father says, and so I'm spending the whole week at the library. For once I want to finish the year with good grades (plus my father promised me that if my average is above an 85, I can visit my aunt in London this summer). Other than doing homework and writing papers, I went to a movie with Orit yesterday. I wouldn't mind seeing it again when you come back. It's called "Star Wars," and I'm totally in love with the hero.

Michalush, I'm glad you haven't gone all religious on me yet, and I can't wait for you to go back to being the old Michali. What's all this nonsense swirling around in your head? And this Simcha guy- you haven't told me whether or not you ended up meeting him. You know, we secular people also leave our doors unlocked sometimes- it's not something the religious people invented. And since when do you think about synagogues and long skirts and yeshiva boys? I hope that when you come back, you're ready to go back to having fun, the way we used to before that seminar messed with your head.

I miss you.

Love,

Tamar

φφφ

During Passover break, I went to the kibbutz with my family. Tamari wanted to come, too, but her grades were down, and her parents wouldn't let her go. At that time, of course, she simply wasn't capable of learning anything; all she could think about was Chagai, Chagai, and more Chagai. I was disappointed. I missed her spirit and her joy.

When I was with Tamari, I could be myself. I could be even better than myself. With Tamari, I felt free to be as silly as I wanted. I gave myself permission to fool around in a way that I wouldn't have dared to do with anybody else. Although I was sorry to miss out on sharing so many experiences with her, I didn't let it ruin my vacation. I spent most of my time at the pool, splashing around in the cool water. Then I'd get out and bask in the blazing sun. My parents went on day trips with my brothers, but I refused to go with them. Vacation meant freedom, I argued, and Passover was all about leaving slavery for freedom, and for me freedom meant hanging out by the pool doing nothing. My parents objected but, as usual, they ended up giving in. My father in particular could never stand his ground, and he caved immediately.

It was very hot, and there were mosquitoes everywhere. That's how it was in the valley at that time of year, and during the summer, too. But it didn't matter. I had all the time in the world, and I could just read one book after another. It wasn't long before I finished everything I'd brought with me, and so I started going to the library to look for new books. I had a lot of free time in the mornings, when my family was traveling and my friends were working- even my cousin Yael, who was a year older than me, worked in the preschool- so I would just sit by the pool and read. By the end of that week, I was almost black, and my nose was starting to peel. Yael, who was my friend as well as my relative, made sure my evenings were never boring. She introduced me to her group of friends, and they welcomed me with open arms. At night we raided the supermarket and helped ourselves to anything we wanted- milk, yogurts, whatever- and feasted on them all night. Then the next morning, nobody could get up.

I loved how free the kibbutz children were; their lives were so different from Aviva's. The kibbutz kids ran up and down the paths, barefoot and in shorts, while Aviva had to wear button-down blouses with elbow-length sleeves even in the height of summer. There were so many prohibitions in her community, so much concern about what other people might think.

If you looked at it from a different perspective, the kibbutz community isn't all that different from the religious community. In both groups, everyone cares about- and meddles in- everyone else's business. I was especially disappointed with Simcha, who didn't even glance in my direction. Maybe he was afraid that I would damage his connection with God, not to mention his social status. It might be dangerous for him to be connected to a secular girl like me. And so my "religious phase" ended, and my "kibbutz phase" began.

I loved the kibbutz. I loved the quiet, the grassy fields, the tall trees, even the old-timers we encountered as we walked along the paths. I liked the way you greeted everyone who walked by- it made me feel at home- and how, in the evenings, the dining hall would be wall-to-wall people and would be buzzing cheerfully. I had no idea how much I would come to love the kibbutz life, and how my memories of it would influence me for so many years to come.

Whenever I went to the kibbutz, I would write to Tamari, and she would write back. I loved her letters. We'd usually write to each other before we even left home, so both of us would find letters waiting for us after we'd said our goodbyes.

April 3, 1981

Chol HaMoed, Passover

Dear Tamari,

I'm still having a blast on the kibbutz. I met some of the older kids, and they're really great. They study, they work, they're tan and tall and good-looking, and they all have blonde hair. You would think the kibbutz produces only blondes. Really. I have no other explanation…. Anyway, it turns out that we all get really hungry at night. Yesterday our whole group, including my cousin Yael and I, raided two of the children's houses and emptied out their fridges. You should have heard what went on the next morning. They called the whole group (including me) in for a serious talk with the kibbutz administrator, and after we confessed our "crime," we got a collective punishment: three nights of kitchen and cafeteria duty. I'm in charge of cleaning the tables- it's harder than it sounds. Actually, the punishment ended up being kind of fun. We didn't mind the work, as long as we got to stay together.

Last night we went to the "youth" dormitory- that's what they call the area where my friends live (without their parents). We sang and played guitar until two in the morning. It didn't make much difference to me, but some of the kids had to get up at five to do their jobs. There are fourteen kids in the group: six girls and eight boys. They all grew up together, and they're like brothers and sisters. The boys and girls sleep in separate rooms and they have separate showers, but other than that they're together all the time, at work and in school. To a city girl like me it looks like heaven, but I've already learned that things aren't always what they seem. Maybe it only looks that way to an outsider. But either way, it's fun, and right now that's what matters.

OK, we'll see each other in a few days. Maybe I'll even see you before you get this letter. And try not to go overboard with Chagai, OK?

Miss you,

Michal

φφφ

June 1982, The Lebanon War. Technically, it was called
"Milchemet Sh'lom HaGalil"- The War for Peace in the North.
Even after all those years, they were still trying to put the word
"peace" into wars. It infuriated me. There was shelling in the
Upper Galil, but here in Herzliya, all we knew about was what we
saw in the papers: descriptions of the battles, death
announcements, photos of beautiful young men who used to be
and are no longer.

That was the summer Tamari went to London, and I missed her
terribly. The dreadful war, which was ravaging so many families,
had hardly touched our community. Here, everything was much
too normal, and life went on as usual. I visited Aviva, hung out at
the beach, spent a week at a kibbutz on a work camp with the
Garin- the group- that Tamari and I had joined, and waited for my
last year of high school to begin. I wanted the war to be over by
the time we got drafted; I didn't want to see any of my friends get
injured, or, God forbid, die. At the same time- and this had
nothing to do with the war- my political views were shifting to the
right. What I valued above all else was my love for my country,
and my commitment to a unified Israel. Geulah Cohen, a right-
wing politician, was revered by many Israelis, and I was certain
that I would vote for her party in the upcoming election. After
hearing her impassioned speeches about the land and the
importance of keeping it whole- values I believed in so deeply- I
decided to join her campaign. Mostly I handed out flyers. My
father and I were bitter enemies. As a leftist and a fervent
supporter of Yitzchak Rabin (and a fervent opponent of Shimon

Peres), he was ashamed of my nationalist views, which in his eyes were a recipe for disaster.

When Tamari returned to Israel, she found out that Oz, her neighbor from the second floor, had been gravely injured. Never again would he be the same light-hearted young man with a great sense of humor. Many months after he returned home from the hospital, she could still hear him crying out the names of his friends in the middle of the night and breaking out into furious tears.

I tried to convince her to support the "Tchiya" party that I admired so much, but she said that politics weren't her thing. She didn't even know who she was going to vote for; this I couldn't understand.

London, she claimed, was "beautiful and dreamy." She couldn't believe that she had persuaded her father to let her go despite her unimproved grades. She had made a good-faith effort until Chanukkah, but once she and Chagai became a couple, she stopped caring about school. Her parents tried all kinds of tricks, including a promise of a summer trip to England. They kept up their part of the deal even though she didn't, and that summer, she went to visit her Aunt Shlomit in London.

Chagai had no choice but to spend the summer without her, and neither did I. She was my other half, and I believe I was hers as well. We were inseparable: we sat together in school, chose the same electives, did our homework together, and went to the same jazz class twice a week in the side street by Drora's shop.

Whenever we visited each other, we'd always walk each other home. Usually at some point we'd sit down on the curb in the middle of the street, chatting as if we had just met. We never ran out of things to talk about. We could laugh about the littlest things, and also lose ourselves in serious philosophical discussions, most of which didn't get us anywhere. My political views may not have interested her at all, but we both believed in freedom and love, and dreamed that someday, when we had children of our own, we would raise them together.

The summer was strange without her. I was lonely, and I waited impatiently for her letters, which arrived almost daily. I wrote to her every couple of days, too. I described, in great detail, what I did, who I met, what I thought and felt; she described her walks around the city streets, her visits to museums and galleries. She couldn't say enough wonderful things about her Aunt Shlomit. This aunt of hers had been living in London for many years, and whenever she came to visit, the only time I would see Tamari was in school. Whenever she had a free moment, she'd spend it with her aunt. Then she would tell me what the two of them did: where they went, what they talked about. Shlomit also provided her adopted daughter with an entire wardrobe of beautiful clothes. None of my relatives lived abroad, and I was always a little jealous of Tamari.

Her visit to her aunt gave her a new perspective on life. Shlomit wasn't married and she didn't have children. She lived in a small apartment in one of London's swankier neighborhoods, and she rubbed shoulders with the most fashionable people. Shlomit introduced Tamari to her friends, and took her all around the town. Tamari was thrilled with her new-found freedom. In

Shlomit's world, "boundaries" were frowned upon, "experiments" became "adventures," and nobody gave a damn about the rest of the world. Herzliya and London were a world apart. Tamari was blinded by the brilliance of everything she saw, and when she talked about the big city, and about her aunt, she didn't leave out a single detail. She was beguiled by the multi-hued world she encountered, by the Indians and Chinese and Pakistanis, by the range of cultures and colors and languages, by the different styles of ethnic clothing, by the scents of exotic foods.

The minute Tamari landed, Shlomit whisked her off to a Chinese restaurant, and it was so good, she said, she was licking her fingers. She'd never had Chinese food before. Shlomit took her for a stroll through the neighborhood, pointing out the nearest Underground station; she bought her a monthly pass and a map of London; she taught her everything she needed to know to make her way around the city by herself. Every evening, they made plans for the following day, and while Shlomit was working, Tamari wandered through the streets, visited museums, soaked up the culture, and learned more English than she'd thought possible.

Tamari reveled in her new-found freedom, and in one of her letters, she wrote that she could hardly wait to be drafted. She'd had enough of both school and home, and she was ready for a new and different life. I was baffled. Not only was I not in a rush to finish high school and go into the army, but I was actually somewhat anxious about it. Life at home wasn't bad, and I had no reason to hurry.

July 12, 1982

21 Tamuz 5742

Greetings to the awesome Tamari,

We're all doing fine, but the war in Lebanon- which for some reason they're calling "The War for Peace in the North"- is still going strong. In the northern towns, life is tough, but here in Kibbutz Eilot, way down in the south, we don't feel anything. I mean, of course we're all glued to the TV and the radio, but that's as close as we get. We're praying it will end soon.

Now, onto our own business: of course I remember our "declaration of love." Like you, I have no doubt that if you were a boy, I would marry you, but the fact is, I just don't find you sexually attractive. It looks like we'll have to be content with a platonic friendship. Oh well, what can you do?

It was wonderful to get your letter. I couldn't believe what a short time it took for a letter from London to travel all the way to the other end of the earth. Anyway, I'll be here for another month or so. I guess you could say that the two of us abandoned the (unsinking) ship on the Mediterranean shores, at least for a few weeks. I hope that when we both get home, we'll still have a chance to go to the beach before it gets too cold. I am very proud of you for being so independent in London. I've never been out of the country, and I can't even imagine how I would feel in a completely foreign place where I didn't understand what the people around me were saying. Do you speak English with your aunt's friends? Do you ever use the English we learned in school?

Write me with all the details, because I'm dying to know what it's like to live somewhere else. How does it feel? What's the weather like? Tell me everything!

We got here- to the southernmost kibbutz in the whole country- three days ago, and it really feels like the end of the world. The desert heat is unbearable, and it's hard to believe that not only can people live here in the summer, but they can work in the fields and the orchards, too. The day starts very early, especially if you're working outdoors. (they put me in the date grove). I'm still not used to getting up at three-thirty in the morning. I work straight through until noon, when we go back for lunch. After that, most people go to sleep, but I'm just waking up. Then in the evenings, when everyone else is going to the pub or hanging out on the fields singing and playing guitar... that's when I crash. Working in the grove is pretty disgusting. I'm supposed to check the irrigation, which means that every so often I get sprayed by a hose full of stinky, recycled water. Yuck! Still, overall it's kind of fun.

It's strange, being so far from home. I still call my family every day from the central telephone, but I haven't felt homesick yet. My mother misses me terribly and even offered to come out for a visit. Obviously, I talked her out of that idea pretty quickly. All I need is for the two of them to show up here with pots full of food....

It's fun to live with friends. The kids from Ashdod are really nice, and so are the kids from Haifa. Remember that girl Anat? We're in the same room. I hope you'll come to the next encampment with me (they've already announced that it will be on Sukkot). And of course, I hope you consider going to Nachal with me. I'm so glad I have the option to serve in Nachal instead of the regular army. How wonderful it will be to go somewhere completely uninhabited, and transform it into a kibbutz or a village! Don't you want to spend your army service working the land? Building something out of nothing?

Anyway, the kids from Tel Aviv are the best, especially D'vir. Remember him? Well, he's a total sweetheart. We'll see what happens. OK, I'm off to send this letter before the office closes for the day.

Write soon! Hugs and kisses, Michal

φφφ

The war went on, with no end in sight. And the longer it went on, the more apathetic we became. Anything that didn't touch us directly was promptly forgotten. The soldiers looked tiny and far away, and I went on with my life as if everything was normal.

The work camp on the kibbutz was the highlight of my summer: a bunch of carefree kids, far from home, hot and sweaty and bubbling over with hormones and romance. Tamari's letters arrived from London, which felt like a whole other world. I missed her, and there was nobody to share my experiences with. The letters we sent each other were the only way to let off some steam.

I was sent to work in the date groves. Everything on the kibbutz was completely upside-down. The day started in the middle of the night; it was hard to get up before the sun. Every morning, as we rode the lurching truck to the date grove, we would watch the sun rise.

Eventually, the work changed, as did the season. Instead of checking the pipes that carried the putrid water, now we were supposed to wrap the dates to keep the bugs from eating the ripening fruit. We climbed up to the highest branches and slipped burlap bags over the fruit. We had heartfelt conversations on those trees, traded gossip, and occasionally had date wars between one tree and another. Our workday ended in the early afternoon; then we'd go back up to the kibbutz and go our separate ways. I would usually explore the scorching roads before heading back to my room near the barn, where I would read until I fell asleep. If I couldn't fall asleep, and my friends were still napping- saving their strength for our evening activities- I would hitch a ride to the beach. This beach wasn't like the beaches I was used to; the water was freezing. But the very fact that I was standing across from a giant body of water made me happy.

That summer I fell in love for the first time, a love that stayed with me for many years, maybe because it was my first love or maybe because afterwards Dan walked into my life, and nothing was ever the same.

That was also the summer I decided to join Nachal. I hoped Tamari would come with me. I loved the atmosphere as well as the people. Mostly, I couldn't see myself sitting in an office and making coffee for the soldiers. Nachal was a chance to avoid both traditional army service and my family. I was ready; I was more than ready. I had never felt any pressing desire to leave home, until now. Something inside me had changed. I felt mature enough to create an independent life for myself, and I couldn't wait to get started.

July 27, 1982

Hey Michalush,

Or as they would call you here, Michelle.

Your two letters arrived today, and I immediately sat down to write back, even though my schedule is booked solid. I hope you appreciate what a sacrifice this is. (Just kidding!) I loved hearing all the gossip about the "Garin". I'm in shock that Yardena is now Tzachi's girlfriend. She's such a loser, and he is so awesome, what can they possibly see in each other? When I tried to imagine Yardena, all solemn and serious, holding Tzachi's hand, I started cracking up. I just can't see it. D'vir is a good guy, and I wish he would just fall head over heels in love with you and kiss you already, because to be seventeen without having kissed anyone yet- well, it just doesn't make sense. You're losing out, there's no denying that, but don't worry, it'll definitely happen. You're the most amazing girl in the world! And I am not- I repeat, not- exaggerating. Don't think for a minute that you are anything less than that!! As my grandmother would say, "Whoever marries you will be a happy man. You're smart, you're nice... what more does a man need?"

I'm still over the moon. London is beautiful, and everywhere I go I discover new and interesting things. I'm in love with the Covent Garden Market, which is kind of like a giant flea market. I bought all kinds of trinkets there, and a white embroidered blouse that is G-O-R-G-E-O-U-S. I'm dying to travel more, to explore other parts of the world. After all, I've only seen one tiny corner of this magical world.

As much as I want to travel, though, the truth is that in the end, I want to go back to Israel. I don't think I could live so far away from my family. The first time I realized that I was missing my family was on Friday night. Shlomit and I went to her friend's house for dinner, and all of a sudden the only place I wanted to be was Grandma's house, welcoming Shabbat. And you won't believe this- I'm having a hard time believing it myself- but I even missed my sister.

It suddenly dawned on me that Shlomit's friends were, in essence, her family. She and I looked at each other, and even though I didn't say a word, I think she knew what I was feeling, because she came over and hugged me, and I hugged her back. It's not that I think she's lonely- she's very busy, and her life is good- but I think that once in a while, even she must miss her parents and my mother.

Poor Chagai writes to me every day and tells me how much he misses me. I miss him, too, and that Friday night I was almost ready to fly back to my family, and to him. But then I saw Nir walking in my direction, and I recovered pretty quickly. Nir is visiting his uncle, who works at the Israeli Consulate, and he is absolutely dreamy. He recently finished his Army service, and the first stop on his "Grand Tour" is London. He's planning to backpack through Europe, then move on to other parts of the world, he's not sure where. Meanwhile, he says he's "conserving energy." He asked me if I wanted to tour Northern England with him next week. I haven't mentioned it to my parents yet, but I talked to Shlomit and she thought it would be OK. (Maybe she needs a break from me!) In any case, Shlomit promised to talk to my parents, and to tell them that Nir is a serious, reliable young man. I haven't told Chagai yet. Maybe it's better if he doesn't find out, so if you bump into him, don't say anything. I wish you were here to help me decide whether or not to go. If I'm lucky, you'll get this letter in time to write back. I wonder what you're going to say. Knowing you, I'm guessing that you're not going to be wild about the idea, but even so, I think I'm going to do it. He's pretty amazing. I'm only here for three more weeks, so why not?

The war is horrible. I hope it ends soon.

Bye for now!

Love,

Tamari

P.S. I really miss the look on your face when I do something shocking. I bet that at this very moment, you're wrinkling up your nose and sticking out your tongue, like you always do when you think I've gone off the deep end!

φφφ

There was one spot on the kibbutz that I loved more than any other: a bomb shelter, with a tall above-ground entrance. If you climbed to the top, you could see for miles. The Edom Mountains and the Red Sea stretched out in front of you, the moon rose between the desert hills, and the skies were cloudless and sprinkled with countless stars. Early in the morning, when the copper-toned sun had risen, heralding a new day, I could climb to the shelter's roof and see the date and mango groves and the melon fields that had been hiding in the darkness of night and were now revealed anew. The sun illuminated the nearby city just as it was beginning to rustle with life. For me, this place was a shelter in every sense of the word. I could sit there by myself, or with a friend. This was where I went to read Tamari's letters. It was utterly quiet and completely still, and whenever one of her letters arrived, I took it straight to the shelter.

Imagine my surprise when I saw D'vir sitting on top of the shelter with Sarit. As though they were waiting for me to come so they could leave. And they did, in fact, hurry away, as if they had read my mind, and I was left alone on the shelter, asking myself, why her and not me? I had fallen in love with him. Not the way you fall in love with someone from afar, when you know you don't really stand a chance, but the way you fall in love with someone just like you, someone your own age. That sense of frustration stayed with me for a long time, until the day he finally noticed me and everything else was history.

After sitting on the shelter roof for a while, trying to calm myself down, I opened the letter. She had written about her day-to-day life, all the trips she took, and our shared dream of seeing the world together, maybe after the army. I found it odd that she'd decided to go to the Lake District in northern England, with an Israeli whom she had met through her aunt. It seemed impulsive and childish, and when I wrote back to her, I urged her to reconsider, but by then- as she had predicted- it was too late. I thought her behavior was so rash, so excessive, that it was actually dangerous. And anyway, she had a boyfriend waiting for her in Israel. For the first time since we'd become friends, I wondered if she was deceiving me as well. Did she always tell me the truth? Perhaps I didn't know her as well as I thought I did.

I told her about my feelings towards D'vir, and about how much I missed her. I even wrote that the "bonding experience" of Kibbutz had been enough for me, and that I'd had all I could take of living so close to other people. I needed to reclaim my personal space.

August 18, 1982

My sweet Michalush,

I'm writing to you because I desperately have to talk to you. Chances are that by the time you get this letter I'll be home, but in case I'm not, I'll tell you what happened. If I don't tell someone, I'll explode.

In the end, I decided to go with Nir. Our trip turned out to be much less hectic than he'd planned. We carried our backpacks with us, and we went everywhere by bus or by hitching a ride. We started out in the middle of the country, then went north to the Lake District. Michali, this trip was a transformative experience for me, for many reasons, one of which is that something really big happened, something huge and unexpected. I have no idea what I'll say to Chagai, Nir just conquered me, in more ways than one. I'll get to that. If I had the patience, I would wait to tell you all of this in person, but I don't, and there's nobody here in London that I can share this with. Yesterday Nir took the night train to Norway, and God knows when I'll see him again. He promised to write, but he'll be gone for at least three months, and I don't really know what's going to happen. You must be bursting with curiosity by now, but don't skip to the end. Read everything in order, it's important. Most of all, don't judge me! I know I can always count on you, but now I need you more than ever.

We started our trip in a city called "Bath." There really is a giant bathhouse there; it was a spa in the time of the Romans. Bath is very romantic, and when you walk through its streets, all you want to do is fall in love, and that's what happened with Nir. He's gorgeous, and he's a gentleman, and he kept dancing around me, making sure I was comfortable and happy. He led me through the ancient ruins and the charming streets, and by the end of the first night I was dying to kiss him. I prayed that I wouldn't have to humiliate myself by kissing him first, and in the end my wish was granted. We were sitting in a small café at the edge of a lake, looking out on the water and talking about ourselves- I told him about the life of a burnt-out student, and he told me about the life of a former paratrooper- and we felt so close to each other, and just as I was about to kiss him, he told me that he couldn't believe I was only seventeen. I corrected him right away, and said, "Almost eighteen." Then nobody said anything for a few minutes. I was so nervous, I started bouncing my leg up and down, and suddenly he looked me in the eye and told me he really wanted to kiss me, and he asked for my permission. He also said he knew I had a boyfriend, but he didn't want to think about him at that moment. The whole time he was talking, he kept looking right at me, and I felt myself sinking into the deep blue of his eyes. For a minute, I wished I hadn't told him about Chagai, who was the last thing on my mind.

I don't think I'll ever forget what we were wearing, or even what he ate or what I drank (I wasn't hungry- when I'm excited, I lose my appetite, and I can hardly even drink. By the end of our ten-day trip I had lost eight pounds). My heart was beating so quickly, and so loudly, I completely forgot who I was or what I was, and I forgot about Chagai, and my arms and legs were shaking , and he reached out and lifted me out of my chair, like I was this fragile treasure, and he pressed his lips to mine. Michali, it was the most amazing kiss I've ever had!!!! And after the kiss, which I wished would never end, we paid the bill and walked up and down the streets and looked in the shop windows. Then we went to the youth hostel- he went to the boys' section, I went to the girls' section- and I was so excited I couldn't fall asleep the whole night, and I really wanted to talk to you about everything that had happened, and I missed you so much.

The next day, we left Bath and headed towards a small village by the sea, where we stayed for four marvelous days. We talked non-stop, and Nir made me laugh and neither of us had much desire to see the sights, we only wanted to get to know each other better, and I wanted the trip to last forever.

After we'd had enough of the muddy English sea, we decided to continue north to the Lake District. We hitched rides, which was a very strange experience. English people are funny, with their accents and their courtesy. They're always happy to give you a ride, they talk about soccer and they tell you that they've been to Israel, or they're planning to go to Israel, or their grandfather on their mother's side was Jewish....

Nir took my hand when we left the hostel and didn't let go all day, and we were holding hands or hugging the whole time, and we were so excited, and all the stars were out, and suddenly Nir's hands started to wander all over my body, and I didn't stop him. I don't really understand what happened next- everything happened so fast. All of a sudden he was lying on top of me, pushing himself into me, and I didn't like it, and I wasn't ready for it, and I whispered, "No," but I'm not sure he heard me, and even if he did, he didn't stop. The whole thing was over in a minute, and there was blood everywhere, and suddenly I felt so embarrassed, and I wanted him to leave, and I gathered my clothes, and I couldn't look at him, and he kept saying, "I'm sorry, I'm sorry, I didn't mean to hurt you, I don't know what came over me, I'm so sorry." And for the rest of the night, neither of us said a word.

When we checked out the next morning, Nir asked for my forgiveness once again. I said that what happened happened, and there's no point in feeling sorry. It wasn't anything like what I imagined the first time would be. But I think I'm glad it was him. We didn't talk about it again, and Nir took care of me as if I were a tiny, delicate baby bird. We still held hands while we walked, but the other kind of "touching," you know what I mean, didn't happen again.

We traveled for another couple of days, and it was fine. Then we went back to London. He continued north, and I'm going back to Israel. Every day since it happened, I keep checking to see if I'm walking differently, or if I look different. I don't think I've changed, at least not on the outside, but you can tell me when I see you. I lost my virginity in England, and I don't know how I feel about it. And I'm going home, and I'll have to tell Chagai that it's over between us, and I'll be starting my last year of high school, and it's all swirling around in my head and I don't even know what I want anymore.

I'm happy to hear that none of our friends are in Lebanon, but remember my neighbor, Ehud Geva? He was badly injured in an ambush. When will this end?

Hope to see you at the airport. I miss you so much.

Me

φφφ

Our last year in high school flew by. After her trip to London, Tamari was never the same. She lost her zest for life, and, I think, her trust in humanity, and to lose your faith at such a young age is awful. The only positive side to her new seriousness was its impact on her grades. She went from being a mediocre student to being at the top of her class. I think her academic success was an effort to compensate for her physical decline. She stopped taking care of herself, broke up with Chagai, and basically lost all interest in boys. Her parents were so surprised by her good grades that they didn't even notice that she was falling apart, but I did. I tried to convince her to go for counseling, but she refused. She blamed herself for what had happened. Her parents figured she had simply become more mature, thanks to her summer trip to London and the independence she was given there. They were glad that in the end, they had decided to let her go. I wonder what they would have done if they knew what had really happened. Would they have gone to the police? Would they have blamed Tamari? Or would they have blamed themselves for letting her go? I don't know the answer, and anyway, it doesn't matter anymore. I don't think she ever fully recovered from that trauma, but she managed to build a life for herself and to keep on going.

Meanwhile, I was going through the opposite process. I had always been a star student, and now I was starting to regress. School, which had always been so important to me, was now very low on my list of priorities. All I cared about now was my Garin.

Between social activities and getting ready for Nachal, I didn't have time for anything else.

When school let out, Mom and Dad called the three of us into the kitchen. They told us they "had to talk about something important." I was terrified, because when my friend Orit's parents had called an emergency family meeting, it was to announce their divorce. Fortunately for me, my fears were unfounded. Instead, my parents asked us to pack our suitcases because in a few hours we were all flying to London and Paris. I had only been on a plane once before, in fifth grade, when my parents bought me a subscription to a kids magazine that came with a pass for a fifteen-minute flight over Herzliya and Netanya.

The trip to Europe will be engraved in my memory forever. Our family was still together at the time: Mom, Dad, and three rambunctious kids. We didn't know that later on, we would lose Dad, and our lives would be forever changed.

I remember how funny my brothers were when we took off. They had never been on an airplane before, and Tomer, who was only eight, was so scared he was farting the whole time. Eyal, who was already fourteen, was squeezing Mom's hand as if he were a little boy. As for myself, I was thrilled beyond words. I loved when the plane took off, and our tiny little country grew smaller and smaller, until it was no bigger than a pinprick. I sat by the window, too excited to read my book: I was so eager to see another world. In my memory, the flight took forever, even though in reality it was less than four hours long. I did manage to write a letter to Tamari, telling her I would have given anything to be sitting on that plane with her instead of with my family. How wonderful it would be to amble through the streets of London and Paris with her, instead of with my noisy brothers.

This journey turned out to be a life-changing experience, not only because it was our first, and last, family trip abroad. Yes, we bonded as a family, but I also learned a lot about myself: who I was where I would choose to live, what kind of life I would create for myself. After this trip, Israel would feel more like my home than ever before.

The memory of London's grey skies stayed with me for many years. I couldn't understand how people could live their lives inside, hiding from the rain, talking about the rain, always waiting for the sun to come out. The sense of alienation was so strong; it felt more sweet than painful. Walking along the endless streets without seeing anyone I knew, hearing a completely different language, and sometimes more than one, too, feeling completely out of place. In a certain way, it was liberating. Surrounded by family, I felt like I could be who I really was, without worrying about what other people would think. With my family, I could be myself. They would accept me and love me no matter what. And my friends weren't there to pass judgment. It was a feeling of freedom, true freedom.

I remember random details: endless rain, bone-chilling cold, aching legs. Sitting on a park bench when the rain let up and eating fresh, warm fish and chips, feeding breadcrumbs to the ducks. A family walking together, carrying small backpacks, a little boy tearfully begging to be carried, a crowded room in a cheap hotel, a sea of unfamiliar faces going in and out of the Underground stations, beggars, noise everywhere, and then, once everyone had fallen asleep, silence. Other images stayed with me, too: a woman sitting on a bench at Madame Tussaud`s, my first musical, scenery, clothing, music, dance, more noise, so much noise, the Tate Gallery, the British Museum, and being together all the time.

I remember myself thinking about the year that had passed and the year to come, and how nothing would ever be the same. Little did I know just how true this would be, or that this would be our last family trip. I couldn't have imagined where life would take me, or the pain I would have to endure.

I thought about leaving home, and I was flooded with sadness and with a new appreciation of the small, colorful enclave in which I'd grown up, and I was scared to become an adult and leave home. And I felt myself missing my family already, even though we'd just spent two weeks together, and I thought about how, one day, I wouldn't be going to school every morning, and Mom wouldn't be waiting for me with a snack after school, and although growing up might be nice, and starting Nachal was exciting, the things I'd always had would be gone. I remember wondering if I'd feel like a stranger in my own house, and decided that no, I'd come home as often as possible. I could never have imagined what was actually going to happen.

And I thought about Tamari, about what happened to her when she took that trip with Nir, how she'd never really been the same, and how I could barely recognize her these days. I thought about how long it had been since I'd seen her laugh or even smile, and how I wanted her to know that I would always love her, I would always look after her, that what happened to her happened to a lot of girls, they just didn't talk about it, and how much did we really know about the girls in our class? Not that much.

53

Suddenly I realized something I had never really thought about before: she was raped. How could I have not seen it earlier? I had to make her understand that it wasn't her fault that he was entirely to blame, that when a girl says "no" she means no! And she had said "no" and he hadn't listened, and that what he did was inexcusable. And I felt so sorry for her. And I thought about how she didn't have to keep it to herself, she shouldn't keep it to herself, the silence must have been killing her. She was the victim, and she had nothing to be ashamed of. And I remember praying that she would heal, and that she would stop blaming herself. So many thoughts, all in a single trip, that took me to another world, and cut me off from everything familiar.

I remember going to the Elysium Castle, how disappointed I was by its poor design, especially because its gardens were so magnificent. After London, we went to Paris, where the streets were very long, and there were extraordinary museums, one of which contained a single, surprisingly small painting of the Mona Lisa looking at me from every possible angle. And on the train back to London, I looked at my family and I wanted to freeze that moment in time, all of us together, and I knew I would remember this moment for the rest of my life. Then it was time to fly home, and a few days later I went off to the kibbutz and to the army. It was the beginning of a new era.

September 20, 1983

Michali,

Greetings from Camp 80. I was drafted five days ago. Six days ago, Chagai came over and brought me a present- a flashlight. He said he hoped that every time I used it, I'd think of him. But I don't feel anything for him anymore. Ever since that thing happened, my heart is like a stone.

I'm five days into basic training, and I hate every minute of it. My commander thinks she's God's assistant, or maybe even God herself. She bullies us, morning and night. Yesterday I forgot my gun in the tent during one of her surprise drills- you know me, I'm not exactly at my best when I get woken up in the middle of the night. My punishment was a week of "arms confinement," which means that instead of being able to lock up my gun, I have to have it on me 24/7- in the bathroom, in the cafeteria, everywhere. Plus, I have to spend the weekend here. She says she's doing me a huge favor by not pressing charges. You'd think I was training to be the commander-in-chief or something. Michali, all I want is for them to leave me alone! Mostly, I want to go home. I swear, I don't understand why they can't let us get any sleep. Will they be able to cram more information into my head if they wake me up at four in the morning? I don't think so.

It's clear to me now that I'm not cut out for the military. I share a tent with all kinds of girls, including a religious girl who wanted to serve in the army instead of just doing national service. You should see how our commander treats her, like she's some kind of hero. I hope you're not going to tell me that you warned me about this and I could have gone to Nachal with you. That's not the right place for me, either, I don't have the patience for "Garin discipline," where everyone has to do the same thing, and you have to get permission from the Garin leaders for every little thing. Yes, it's too bad we're not together, but all things considered, I don't regret my decision. I hope they'll let me do something interesting, but I'm not ready to commit myself to anything yet, so I still don't know where I'll be. I do know that I'd rather sit at home the whole day than do something boring.

What's going on with you? I didn't even ask.

Write back to me at Camp 80.

See you at some point, if the commander allows it. Any chance you'll surprise me and come for the weekend?

Love you forever,

Tamar Tzadok, ID # 3287731, property of the Israeli Army.

φφφ

She sent me three letters, and I didn't answer any of them. She even left me a few messages at the kibbutz office, but I didn't call her back. She wrote about what her life was like in the army, but all I could think about was how angry I was that she had abandoned me. We were supposed to be on the Nachal track together, but she decided to do the regular army track instead, because "the gang," as she called it, was pressuring her to do so. She made this decision at the very last minute, and I took it badly. I was angry and offended. I had been there for her all year, when she was having such a hard time. How could she leave me now?

Among other things, she wrote that Nir had come back from his travels and hadn't gotten in touch with her. After everything that had happened, I couldn't understand how she could think about him at all, much less want to see him. The whole idea sickened me, and I couldn't write or talk to her. In her third letter, she asked if I'd forgotten her entirely. Then she stopped writing. After a few months, the distance between us became intolerable. Maybe our relationship wasn't beyond repair. And so, as hard as it was, I made myself write back to her. And I'm glad I did. From that point on, our friendship was stronger and more loving than ever, and it continued that way for many years, until the incident that severed us completely. After that, I didn't want to hear her name ever again.

October 23, 1983

Hey Tamari,

After weeks of debating with myself, I've decided to write to you. Yes, you're right: I have been avoiding you, and the fact that we haven't talked in so long isn't just accidental. At first I thought that it would be better if we spoke in person, but between the hassle of leaving the kibbutz and your "outstanding army service," getting together wasn't so easy, and now you're in a special course and you have no idea where you'll be posted. (Just between us, I'm glad the army is investing in you. Your mother said that you've decided to give the army a chance, and vice versa. What can I say? I hope things work out this time around.)

Yes, I am hurt and insulted. Three months ago, when you took the midnight bus out of the kibbutz, I had to stop myself from blurting out what I thought about our friendship in general, and about you in particular. But now I think it's time to speak frankly. Maybe it's better that you're not here and that I have to express myself in writing. I'm picturing the look on your face as you read this letter, and I know that reading it won't be easy for you, but as hard as it might be, the time has come to speak the truth. Believe me, writing this letter isn't so easy, either. Anyway, I hope this introduction doesn't scare you away, and that you'll be able to take in what I'm about to tell you.

This past year was a difficult and confusing one for you, but I stood by you every step of the way, even at your hardest, most desperate moments. I didn't leave your side, not for a minute.

58

When we decided to go into Nachal, it was a joint decision: we would go through the army together. Of course I would remain by your side, just as I always had, and I assumed you would stay by my side, too. But you had other ideas, and you weren't even honest and fair enough to let me in on them, and so the first time someone got on your nerves, as the head of the Garin punished you and Itzik for going on a hike without permission, even though you knew you'd be missing a seminar. You didn't like what the Garin had to say, so you went back to your room, let out a string of curses, packed up your bags, and took the midnight bus home.

What were you thinking?

You didn't check with me; you didn't even ask for my opinion. What am I, invisible? Turns out you never even bothered to change your draft date, so that you'd be drafted with the rest of us. How come I didn't know that? You didn't tell me anything. You just left! What kind of friend are you anyway? Then you send me this letter about how hard basic training is and how Nir is in the country and he didn't get in touch with you, and you can't understand why I don't write back, and you can't imagine why in the world I might be angry with you. All I can say now- after all your letters- is that I don't understand. You call yourself a friend? You can't see two inches past your own nose! You never think about anyone else, not even for a second. I've had enough of your self-pity. What about me? Don't you see that you betrayed me? You left me alone. I'm sharing a room with Vered now, and it's fine, but you and I were supposed to be together.

I'm very angry with you, and it will take me a long time to get over it. So keep your distance.

I called your house, and your mother gave me your address at the course. I hope you get this.

Michal

November 2, 1983

Hey Michalush,

It's already Tuesday, two days after I came back to the kibbutz, and I'm so glad I did, even though it meant traveling from one end of the country to the other. So many hours of travel, almost as long as the flight to America, but it was worth it. Our friendship is one of the most important things in my life, and if it takes a trip across the country to preserve it, so be it.

Sometimes I can be so dense. Like you said, I can't even see beyond my own nose. But you have to promise that no matter how angry you might get, you will never, ever cut me off.

I got your letter in the evening, after an exhausting day of classes. When I saw the envelope with your name on it, I was elated, but once I started reading it, I started to cry. What an idiot I've been. I didn't think about you at all. It was so selfish of me to leave like that without asking you how you felt. I don't know what got in to me. I couldn't think about anything other than how much I wanted to get out of that prison.

After I read your letter, I almost went AWOL. All I could think about was seeing you and telling you how sorry I was. I hoped and prayed for your forgiveness. Lucky for me- or maybe not so lucky- the course I told you about, which is very hush-hush, is in a hole somewhere, and the only way in and out is by the army car, and the bus station is so far away, there's no way I could leave even if I tried. I had to wait a day and a half, until Thursday afternoon, when I could finally get a lift to Tzfat's central bus station. It was a nightmare for me, having to wait so long. All I could think about was you, and what I would say to you, and what you would say to me, and I kept imagining our conversation, and I couldn't sleep a wink, much less concentrate on my studies.

When Thursday finally came, I took the bus from Tzfat to Haifa, where I waited two hours for the midnight bus. When I finally got to your kibbutz, I ran to the children's house to find you, but you weren't there. Then I met Chen from the "Youth" section, who told me you were in the storage closet, and I went to find you there, and you didn't hear me come in, but I could tell that you were in another world because you had that glass-eyed look you get when you're daydreaming. Then when you finally saw me, you asked me what I was doing there, and you didn't sound the least bit angry, just surprised. Then everything I was planning to say instantly flew out of my head, and instead I just mumbled, "Sorry." As much as I had imagined what I would say, and what you would say back and as worried as I was that you wouldn't even want to talk to me, in the end I just burst into tears and you came over and hugged me. We went outside, and we talked non-stop just like we used to, and we didn't stop talking all weekend, and we must have walked around the kibbutz ten times, and we hardly slept, and you managed to get out of the Garin activities and hang out with me instead, which I'm sure wasn't so easy and on Saturday night you walked me to the bus and I went back to the course without even stopping at home (luckily I was able to use the kibbutz laundry). And now my mother is angry that I didn't stop by to see her, but I'm not too worried, you know my mom, she always forgives me. And anyway, I promised her I would be home next week, and so would you, and the two of us would sit with her until she threw us out of the house.

So here I am, back at this high-pressure course. It's very stressful, but it's interesting. And after surviving my horrible experience in basic training, where I felt like a cog in some kind of screwed-up wheel, nothing seems quite so terrible, and maybe in the end, the army won't be so terrible, who knows?

But like I told you when I saw you, the Garin is not for me. All day long, everyone's on top of each other. That's not my thing. I wish it hadn't turned out that way, but the bottom line is, I just couldn't take it anymore. Two months in this hole hasn't just wiped me out, it's also made me lose my mind. I've even started smoking. I am so sorry that you felt abandoned- you know that wasn't my intention. You also known that I'm an impulsive person. If something doesn't suit me, goodbye and good luck. At least I didn't try to drag you with me. I hope things continue to go well for you, even though they've taken you out of the children's house now that the caretaker is all better. I can't believe they put you in the laundry room with all the old fogies. I salute you for your patience, and for the way you accept whatever comes your way. I could never do that. But the fact that we're so different is one of the best things about our friendship. Maybe that's why we're never bored when we're together.

Take care of yourself, and see you at home,

Your loving friend,

Tamari

ФФФ

Before we were officially drafted into Nachal, we went through an orientation period. For me, it flew by. It didn't take me long to get used to kibbutz life. I loved the routine, I loved being with my friends, I loved walking barefoot (when the ground wasn't blisteringly hot), and most of all- I was in love. I was head over heels in love with D'vir, but I didn't have the guts to tell him. He worked in the fields and I worked in the children's house. We'd see each other at meals, and we'd walk through the kibbutz together, but he had no idea that for me, this was more than just a friendship. His curly hair, his charming smile, and his endless optimism won me over, and I would frequently catch myself daydreaming about him, praying that he would take the first step.

The boys were drafted before us, so we ended up staying on the kibbutz by ourselves for a few months, where we went through basic training. Living in tents, in the middle of the winter, wasn't much fun, but at least we weren't bothered by the heat and the mosquitoes. I guess it's true, what they say: every cloud has a silver lining. It was hard to get up on those frigid mornings, to climb out of our warm beds into the ice-cold tents which we could never manage to seal completely. Aside from that, it wasn't that terrible.

The support of our fellow Garin members made a huge difference. Basic training was much easier when you were going through it with your closest friends. It made the most difficult parts a little more tolerable. For me, the worst part was weapon training. I had no interest in weapons. I had no interest in firing a gun, in killing, in hurting another person, in fighting for something, or against something. It was all completely alien to me.

During weapon training, we would sit in small groups, and our commander would teach us about all the parts of the gun, how to use a gun, how to clean it. I couldn't concentrate; in fact, I had to stop myself from laughing when I looked at my friends in their army caps, looking like tiny, harmless turtles.

There were two groups, two Garins in our training unit: mine, and another group of girls from a boarding school. After a while we realized that one of the girls from the other group was stealing from just about all of us. Some of the girls in that group snuck out every night to meet their boyfriends, who were staying at a nearby kibbutz. Once, I remember, we were all supposed to spend the weekend on the kibbutz. The girls in the other Garin spent hours poking tiny holes in their skin to make it look like they had scabies. Of course, they got to go home while the rest of us stayed on the base, miserable. Sometimes they refused to pull their weight, and we had to do everything ourselves, which ended up making our own Garin even closer. Once in a while, the whole group would assemble, and we'd finally get to see the boys. We couldn't wait for those meetings. Mostly I wanted to see D'vir. I was eager to move on to the settlement phase, which followed basic training. Then, he and I would be together, working the land, and maybe even becoming a couple. Which is, of course, what happened.

Tamari continued down her chosen path until she'd had enough. The crisis came to a head when one day when, without any warning, she showed up at the kibbutz and immediately fell apart.

January 28, 1984

You'll never guess who I saw. Of all the soldiers in the country, who has a reserve service, who do you think was sent here? Nir! Like I told you, our unit takes people from all the divisions, including his. Can you imagine? I'm on my way to the kitchen, and all of a sudden, there he is! A real fata morgana. I didn't know whether to laugh or cry. I could tell from his expression that it took him a minute to recognize me. When I finally managed to croak out a greeting, he said, with a huge smile on his face, "Hey, look who's here! I can't believe it! Hello, little girl!" He called me "little girl." How dare he call me that, after he stole my girlhood from me? My heart was beating a mile a minute and my knees started to buckle. I collapsed onto a nearby rock. Nir laughed; he must have thought I was overcome with joy. Maybe he even fantasized that I was still in love with him. Anyway, he sat down next to me and started telling me all about the last few months, how he'd just gotten back from "the trip of a lifetime," that he's working on his college applications and hopes to start at the Technion University in the fall. He talked about himself non-stop, and he complimented me, saying how good I looked in a uniform, but he didn't bother to ask me how I was doing or how I felt, and he wasn't the least bit interested in what my life had been like for the past year and a half. I told him I was in a rush, and he said he was, too, but we'd see each other later, and I mumbled some response and ran off.

I had a double shift of guard duty- one of the girls had to go home because her father was sick- so I was able to dodge him for a while. Now I'm back in the girls' barracks, and I'm scared to leave. If only you were here... All of a sudden, I feel like everything is just too hard. I can't look at his face again. My stomach is turning upside-down; I just want to go home. I'm starting to think that I'll never leave this room, I'll just stay here until my next shift. But what if he comes looking for me? I could ask my bunkmate, Efrat, to tell him I'm not here, but this place is so small, that would never work.

I want to die, it's that simple. I can't stop crying. It's all coming back to me, as if it just happened yesterday. How do I make it stop? Why aren't you here? OK, I have to pull myself together. I think you're right, I really do have to talk to someone, but who? I'm stuck here at the end of the world, in the middle of nowhere. I'm cut off from everyone. Michal, I have to see you. I know you're finishing up basic training, and your commencement ceremony is in ten days. I have to be there.

Love you and miss you, Me

2005

Looking back after all these years, I still can't figure out exactly when everything started to fall apart between me and D'vir. I had been in love with D'vir. We'd been together for three years, maybe more, we'd backpacked through Europe together, and we were even thinking about moving in together. But then, out of nowhere and without any warning, I started to see him a little differently. You know what I mean, like when you look at someone very close to you and all of a sudden that person seems like a stranger. In addition- perhaps as a result- I couldn't see us as parents, and I knew I wanted a family. What kind of father would D'vir be? After all, he was pretty immature. Charming, yes, but shallow. Our temporary arrangement seemed like it could go on forever, and I didn't want it anymore.

D'vir's smooth façade seemed to be ironed on permanently, and it was starting to bother me. He had a simple solution for every problem, but I saw things differently. I didn't see the world as black and white, and I didn't think the easiest solution was necessarily the best. In the beginning of our relationship, all I wanted to do was get up in the morning, pack up his guitar, a tiny tent, and a few cans of food, hitch a ride to the Kinneret, and sprawl on the beach. That had been my idea of paradise. Now, it seemed somewhat irresponsible to ride with all these strange drivers, some of whom drove so quickly and carelessly that you'd think they were trying to commit suicide right there on the road. D'vir found my uneasiness amusing. He'd survived Lebanon, he said, and he wasn't about to worry about driving on the Akko-Tzfat highway, even if there was a disturbed driver at the wheel.

Now, sunbathing on the beach felt like a waste of time. At first I tried to remember our shared past: how madly in love I was, how close we were. It helped for a little while, but invariably my doubts would return. I was exhausted.

On top of everything else, I was starting to think about going back to school. D'vir believed that formal education was both useless and oppressive, that you could learn everything you needed to know from books, that you didn't need a certificate to prove your intelligence. You could learn everything by yourself, he argued, and as long as you hungered for knowledge, you were your own best teacher. He believed that teaching yourself directly, without any intermediaries, was the truest kind of learning.

D'vir cultivated a group of disciples who worshipped the ground he walked on. They would have followed him through fire and water. Most of them were from our Garin; a few were from the army, a few from his string of temporary jobs. I had no patience for these people, wherever they were from. They had no interest in money, and for them, work was just a way to support themselves while they cavorted around the world, playing music. Money wasn't the most important thing for me, either, but I knew that it was something you needed if you wanted to live comfortably, and that before you could plan a future, you had to think about securing an income.

I couldn't envision a future for us, and one day I just told him that I thought we should break up. D'vir couldn't understand: we loved each other, why wouldn't we want to stay together? I told him I no longer loved him (even though I did), and that it was over. End of story.

The moment I decided to cut him out of my life, I tried to uproot every sign of him. I severed all my connections with mutual friends, I didn't answer his phone calls, I stayed out of his neighborhood. I didn't want to hear about him or talk about him. I put him in a box, sealed it tight, and set it aside.

I enrolled in an occupational therapy program at Haifa University, and shortly after the start of the school year, I was dating Dan, an undergraduate student in computer science. Dan was the antithesis of D'vir. What I loved about him was how much he thought about the future, how carefully he planned everything. Dan had figured out his whole future, one move at a time, and I was one of the squares on his chessboard. I knew I could count on him to do all the planning, to take charge; in essence, I went from being pulled by one cart to being pulled by another. I had been in two serious relationships in my life, and I had never set the tone in either of them. I was just dragged along.

φφφ

The days that followed were a nightmare for her. She tried to avoid Nir, but wherever she went, he came looking for her. He even had the nerve to go into the girls' barracks. She was constantly upset, and had trouble focusing. She didn't leave the room unless she absolutely had to, not even to go to the dining hall; her friends brought her food. If she spotted Nir, she would turn away, praying that he wouldn't see her. She was afraid of him and of herself as well. She was too scared to confront him, to make him realize how much he had made her suffer.

As miserable as she was, the thought of charging him with rape never even crossed her mind. She didn't understand what had happened; perhaps she chose not to understand. I try to remind myself that things were different back then; the whole idea of rape was taboo. Nobody wanted to think about it. Anyway, after I got that awful letter from her, I was able to get a one-day pass to visit her at her base. I think I managed to convince her that it wasn't her fault but his. He's the one who should have been running away. I even made her smile a couple of times. But after 24 hours I had to go back to my base, and once again, she was alone. In the end, he left, and she tried to get back to her routine. I think it must have been around then that she decided to enlist in an officers' course. Why else would someone like her, who hates restrictions of any kind, especially those related to the army, choose to enroll in an officers' course? She even signed on for a few extra years of army service.

Personally, all my memories from this part of my life are good ones. The boys returned to Camp 80 at the end of basic training, which spiced things up a lot. Officially, we were only allowed to see each other on special occasions, but we always found a way to meet up anyway, and the fact that these meetings were illicit made them all the more exciting. I managed to see D'vir almost every day, and on the last Friday, a few days before our ceremony, I got a note from him saying that if we both got leave that weekend, we should go to the kibbutz together. In the end we had to stay on the base, but I was thrilled nonetheless. Could it be that after so many years of being invisible, I was finally becoming a significant part of someone else's life? I hoped so with all my heart. That note kept me going for several weeks, even though we only became an official couple after we moved to the settlement.

My parents, my brothers, and even my grandmother came to my commencement ceremony. Every detail of that evening is engraved in my memory. Dad was still with us, and life seemed so simple. D'vir was starting to pay attention to me, and I felt like I had won the lottery. I felt independent and strong, and above all, I was exhilarated at the prospect of spending the next six months on the pioneer settlement with D'vir. I was filled with all the hopes and expectations and dreams of a young girl in love.

She came to the ceremony, too. It occurred to me that she might be jealous; maybe she even regretted her decision to leave our Garin. Throughout all these years, she has vigorously defended her impulsive choice, but I'm still not convinced. If she was so sure of her decision, why would she feel the need to keep justifying

herself? Once again, I doubted her integrity, and once again I
chose to suppress my feelings and fight for our friendship.

In her letter, she wrote:

It was very moving to see your family at the ceremony. Your
father tried to hide his tears, and your mother was shooting
photos non-stop, babbling the whole time. Every five minutes,
she'd comment on how beautiful you looked, how proud she was,
how your brothers were so emotional. I looked over at them, and
I thought about how nice it must be to have a family as wonderful
and unified as yours. No matter what happens, they'll always be
there for you, unconditionally and without judgment.

My mother always makes me feel like a nuisance, a troublemaker.
She's constantly reminding me of all the sacrifices she's made,
and will continue to make, for me, and she never misses an
opportunity to compare me to my sister Maya. When I came back
from England, she didn't even notice that I was depressed. She
thought I was just being a hot-headed adolescent, and the best
thing she could do was wait for it to pass. She tries not to talk to
me about anything serious. In fact, I think she tries to avoid me
altogether.

As for my father, he is so absorbed in his "extremely important
work" that he hardly notices anything else. I'm sure he's not
particularly proud of me, but he's so wrapped up in his own affairs

that he doesn't really think about me at all. I'm not talking about my grades or my military rank- those things have always interested him- but about me, myself: who I am, whether or not I'm happy, what I feel, what causes me pain. He cares a lot about superficial things that don't require any kind of emotional effort, but when it comes to feelings, he's like a turtle retreating into his shell. He's proud of my sister: she was an officer, and now she's a student at the Technion. He's constantly comparing us: she's the successful one, I'm the troublemaker. But you know what? I don't give a damn.

It's strange: as I'm writing this, I'm beginning to see my family in a very different light than I did when I was living at home. We're all floating in our own little bubbles. My sister Maya moved out; she comes home every couple of weeks for Friday night dinner, and everything is calm and orderly. But your house is always full of noise and food and people coming and going, full of life. You write that your mother is very controlling, but she is also involved. She cares about you. Maybe that's how you should think of it.

My life looked picture-perfect compared to hers. Again, I found myself thinking that she should never have left Nachal, but I tried to move on. It was time for me to focus on myself. And anyway, there was nothing I could do for her that I hadn't already done.

March 3, 1984

Tamari,

We haven't gone home for almost a month- pretty much since we got to this "hole," as you would call it, in the middle of nowhere. To our complete surprise, they sent us to a brand new kibbutz right on the border, which is said to be at the foot of Mount Nevo. You know the mountain where Moses stood before he died. God had told him that he would never set foot in the land of Israel; all he could do was look down at the land from the top of the mountain. To get to the settlement, you have to go down the mountain road until you get to Kibbutz Almog; then you continue down a gravel road, turn left, and cross through Beit Ha'A'rava. There is nothing here, nothing at all. My mother said it reminded her of that song, "To the right and to the left, nothing but sand." She's right. My parents came to visit last week, and my mother wanted me to get into the car with her and go back home. I'm sure she's already tried to convince my commander to transfer me to another base closer to home....She's amusing and annoying at the same time. Either way, nothing can keep her from trying. She'll do whatever she can to bring me back home.

The site itself is completely empty, aside from a few barracks, a central office, and a mess hall. And- surprisingly- a small menagerie of farm animals: a few ducks, some rabbits, a pompous turkey who struts around as if he were a peacock. We're really creating something out of nothing, and it's exciting to be starting from scratch. Our goal is to transform the Nevo region into a verdant and blooming place, and eventually into a kibbutz. Every morning, when I wake up in this beautiful setting, a wonderful thought comes into my mind: this is real Zionism, and we are real

75

pioneers. The thought that we are building up something new-that one day there will be children running around- makes me want to do everything I can to make this place beautiful. And that's one of the main reasons I wanted to do Nachal. I feel like I'm doing something meaningful and interesting and completely different than anything I've ever done before.

Getting our room assignments was pretty unpleasant. Some of the girls had already decided who they wanted to room with, and I wasn't prepared for that. It worked out fine in the end. I'm sharing a tiny little room with Dana and Nira, who have been very nice. There's one single bed pushed up right next to a bunk bed. I took the top bunk, hoping it would give me a little more privacy.

Life here is run like a small kibbutz (aside from the military parts, like roll-call- ugh!). Most of our work is here, on the outpost itself: paving roads, working in the kitchen, gardening, taking care of the animals. We also work in some of the other outposts in the region, and any money we earn goes into a special settlement fund. (At some point, we'll decide what to do with it.) There's also a constant rotation of guard duty- we're right on the border, so someone has to be standing guard twenty-four hours a day.

I love the desert. The nights are chilly, but the days are warm and pleasant, and it hardly ever rains. A few days ago, I saw the most beautiful sight of my whole life, in more ways than one!

The moon was full. We had turned off all the lights and were watching the moon rise over the Edom Mountains. It was breathtaking. I felt like I could just reach out and touch it, that's how close it looked. It was gorgeous, and it made me think about Moses, and how he could only see one side of the mountain while the moon illuminated the other, and what a tremendous loss that was for him. And there I was, daydreaming about these lofty matters, about Moses and Mount Nevo, and we were all sitting on the brand new sidewalk that we had just paved a few days ago, and all of a sudden I felt someone taking my hand. It was D'vir! I sat there, frozen, not knowing what to do. Of course, my heart was pounding faster than ever. After a while, I slid my hand out of his and leaned down on my elbows, and he turned to Yael, who was sitting next to him, and started talking to her as if nothing had happened. When I got up to leave, he said, "Hey, Michal, I hear you're the runner tonight. Come by and visit, OK?" It was finally my turn to be the runner- the person in charge of bringing food and drink to the guards, to keep them awake. Did he think I would miss an opportunity like this? I'd been waiting a whole month to "visit" him on guard duty, so I could be alone with him!

All night, I ran from one post to another, bringing the guards coffee and cake that I had baked myself. (Believe it or not, there are actually runners who make French fries for the guards! How can anyone get up for guard duty in the middle of the night and eat French fries?) One of my responsibilities was making sure that the guards were awake, and that they were all at their proper posts. D'vir had been scheduled for the last shift, right before dawn, and when I went to check on him, everything went perfectly. Finally, just the two of us! Without all the noise and commotion, without worrying about what everyone else would say, just us. We talked about all kinds of things: his family, the other kids, our plans for the future. Neither of us mentioned anything about his hand reaching for mine. The next thing we knew, the sun was coming up; his shift was over. He went back to get ready for the day ahead, and I went back to my room where I slept a delicious, dreamless sleep.

And there you have it. I'm flying! We'll just have to wait and see what (if anything) develops.

I'm coming home next weekend. Hope you are, too. If you are, maybe we can go to Sidney Alley Beach, (If it's not raining, of course.). I haven't been there in a long time!

Love you and miss you,

Michal

φφφ

A few weeks later, Tamari was recommended for the officers' course. Her first reaction was to burst out laughing. "They've gotta be kidding," she said. The officers' course was highly structured, and full of rules, and Tamari couldn't stand structure and rules. She also had nothing but contempt for the green uniforms that in her opinion, made "everyone exactly the same." She was surprised that she hadn't already been kicked out of the army; the last thing she expected was to be nominated for an officers' course. Tamari, a career soldier? When she asked why they had nominated her, her officer told her that she had some potential, and that she should give his offer "serious consideration." For an entire week, she didn't share this new development with anyone, not even her parents; she just walked around with all kinds of thoughts stewing in her head. I think she kept it to herself because of the role she played in the family dynamic. Unlike her older sister, who was an officer and therefore a "success," Tamari was considered a loose cannon. If she told them about the offer, they would pressure her to attend the course, and if she decided not to, she knew just what they would say: "there she goes again, sabotaging herself as always." She didn't want them to pressure her; she wanted the decision to be hers alone. And the fact that Nir was on her base made the thought of escape all the more appealing.

We had a chance to talk that week, and I tried to understand how someone so rebellious could even consider signing up for the course. But the truth is, the situation she was in at the time was becoming increasingly restrictive, and she felt like she couldn't breathe. She didn't get along with the other girls- she hated their pettiness and self-righteousness- and she was tired of the boys' tireless attempts to "take it to the next level." None of them interested her, and she became more and more isolated. She had nobody to talk to, to share her feelings and experiences with. She was finding her tiny, overcrowded army base so oppressive that she began reading, something she would never have done had she not felt so desperate. And so, despite her aversion to rules and regulations, she accepted the offer. I think that by then, something inside her was already broken, and as the years went by, she became less rebellious and more conformist.

Enrolling in the course was her best exit strategy, and when the course was over, she was transferred to another base.

May 10, 1984

Michali, I did it. Without consulting my parents or anyone else, I told Roni, my commander, to sign me up for the officers' course. I'm pretty nervous, but I think I'm doing the right thing. I hope so, at least. I made my final decision when I came back here on Sunday. Why Sunday, you ask?

Because the minute I set foot in the base, I could hear people whispering, "Here comes the sociopath." I had to laugh, because the one who was doing most of the whispering is the mother of all sociopaths. She always finds a way to get the best shifts for herself and her mafia. She is such an operator, it's sickening. I looked her straight in the eye, and even though I didn't say a word, she averted her gaze and ran away as fast as she could, a small victory. That's when I knew for sure that I needed a change.

Roni said he was surprised at my decision, but he promised to get me into a course that starts in less than a month.

What else? It was great to see you again, this time just you and me, without anyone else.... Maybe you don't mind having other people there with us, but I do. It's not that I don't like D'vir, it's just that every now and then I want you all to myself. It was wonderful spending the weekend with you and you alone. Even if all we did was sit in the sun, stuffing our faces. I like your mother so much. She tries so hard to make people happy, to pamper them.... Do you think I can borrow her for a little while? When I go home for the weekend, my mother won't even do my laundry, because she doesn't have the time or the energy. I have to tell my parents about my new plan; I'm sure it will make them very happy. Finally, I'll be bringing them a little bit of gratification.

OK, gotta go, I just wanted to keep you in the loop. You're the first one to hear about the course.

Who knows when we'll see each other again?

Tamari

May 20, 1984

Hey Tamari,

What's up? I'm sitting here after a night of guard duty, and I'm wiped out. I only had one hour's sleep before I began my shift at two in the morning. I have four more hours of guard duty, then I can go home

Today I worked in Jahir, Kibbutz Mitzpeh Shalem's watermelon grove. We spent the entire day weeding. There were more weeds than watermelons, which is why my left hand (the one I used for weeding) is all green and calloused and full of cuts, and my right hand is lady-like and delicate.

After dinner, I went with Yael to visit the boys at the checkpoint. When we got there, they were in the middle of preparing an "Immortal Dinner," so we joined in the celebration. We were able to hitch a ride back to Beit Ha'Arava, but we couldn't get back to our own outpost until eleven. When we finally got back, we joined a group of girls singing in the lounge. Then we stayed up talking. As you can see, I didn't get much sleep last night.

Tamari, I'm in love, like I've never been in love before. And this time, for a change, it's mutual. D'vir is wonderful and kind and smart and romantic- the kind of guy I've always dreamed of. Every time our eyes meet, I get a shiver down my spine. I can't get over the fact that he loves me back, and I almost have to pinch myself to make sure I'm not dreaming. I had gotten so depressed, I was sure it would never happen. It's not like he's had all these girlfriends or that he's some kind of Don Juan, but he's available, and all the girls look up to him, so why me?

I ask myself that a lot, but the only answer I can come up with is that I shouldn't ask so many questions. I should just enjoy it for what it is, and that's exactly what I'm doing. The beginning of our relationship came straight out of a fairy tale- I know I've told you this a million times already, but I'm going to tell you again.... How he came and sat down next to me when the moon was rising, how he reached out and took my hand, how I was the runner that night and we sat together for hours and talked. And how, when I woke up and found that his shift was over, we went to breakfast together, and we walked together towards the commanders' swimming pool, where he kissed me. I couldn't believe what he said next: "Have I ever told you that I'm crazy about you?" I was flattered and amused- was he really talking to me? But since then, we've been together, "stuck to each other like glue," according to our friends. I call him "D'virbee" and he calls me "Mickimee ," and it's just so sweet.... I'm reeling from happiness, and I just wish that the next four months would never end. That's when D'vir goes to Unit 50 and the girls go on to the farming unit- we're still not sure exactly where we'll be. What I am sure of, though, is that we won't be spending every day together. Every day and every night. The girls and boys have separate sleeping areas, but I've managed to sneak into his room a few times, when one of his bunkmates is out on guard duty or a military drill. So far, we're just sleeping together- literally. Nothing more.

The settlement is getting prettier every day. Two days ago we planted flowers by the dormitories, and trees along the path from the lounge to the dining hall. It makes things more colorful. Meanwhile, not a single raindrop has fallen, so we're watering constantly. Who knows, maybe at some point it will start to rain.

OK, enough of the serious stuff. Onto the lighthearted, entertaining bits (I don't want to bore you, and you must be dying to hear them) about Anat Ashkenazi. Yael had told me that Anat was a card-carrying liar, but I was never sure, until today!

Last night, I asked her for a roll of toilet paper (the rarest and most coveted item around). She told me she was sure she had some. I followed her back to her room, where she took some out of her purse and handed it to me. I thanked her. End of story.

But this morning, I needed more toilet paper. Since she wasn't in her room, I decided to be proactive and take it myself. Later in the afternoon, when Anat came back from working outside, I asked her, again, for toilet paper. She said, "Oh, you know, yesterday, after I gave some to you, another fifty people must have come to me with the same request. Now I have nothing left." I thought it over for a minute, and realized, to my astonishment- or maybe not to my astonishment- that either I'm an idiot or one of us was lying... and it wasn't me. I asked her if she was sure, and she rambled on for a while, then said yes, she was positive. I didn't argue with her; instead, I decided to check it out myself. I went back to her room, and guess what I found in her purse? Half a roll of toilet paper! What a liar!!!! I caught her red-handed. And what was her crime? Stealing a lousy roll of toilet paper! On my way to work I realized how foolish I was being: she was a liar, and stealing from a liar wasn't really a crime. So later that evening I went back to her room and took whatever toilet paper was left (the first time I've stolen anything in my entire life). Now she's really out of toilet paper, and hopefully she'll learn her lesson.

That's the whole story!

I hope I made you laugh. I miss you so much. Come and visit me already! How can I tell you stories about our settlement if you've never even seen it?

Love,

Mickimee

2005

Sometimes I catch myself daydreaming, and wishing. Wishing we were just another regular family. A family that goes for a drive on a Saturday morning: a father, a mother, and two children, heading down to Lake Sammamish, imagine us bringing our bathing suits and our beach towels, some snacks, some fruit. It's a scorching summer day. We don't have air conditioning at home, but it's always nice on the beach. We meet up with friends. The kids play- a little bit with us, but mostly with each other. You look at me, taking such pleasure in my presence, the way you used to, back when I still believed you, when I still believed in you. I miss the sounds of love. I miss the sounds of children arguing: "Mom, tell him," "Come on, it wasn't me, she started it...." I miss my children's smiles, the touch of their bodies on mine. I feel empty. I am a mother whose two children are inaccessible, out of reach. My children are in another world, and who can tell if the two worlds will ever meet? After all, I abandoned them, and that is unforgiveable. I wrap myself in my sheets; I don't even know what to wish for anymore. A twisted thought passes through my head: perhaps it would have been better if I never had children.

I ask myself, what would have happened if.... What would have happened if I had kidnapped my children, uprooted them from the place they were born and raised, where their parents didn't speak the language, but they themselves were fluent? A place where they knew the rules, where the landscape- so foreign to me- is the landscape of their childhood. What would have happened if I had kidnapped them and brought them to live with me, here, in this country, in the land of their forefathers? What if I refused to return them to their father? What if I hadn't imprisoned myself inside myself?

I think about them all the time, wondering if moving here, alone, was the right decision. Then I get sucked into a lengthy debate between me and myself, two seasoned lawyers representing the two opposing parties: for and against bringing them here without their father's permission, for and against bringing them here against their will. For and against bringing them here because it is a mother's prerogative. Would it have been morally acceptable to bring them? To leave them behind? Is severing the connection more effective when it hurts? These debates leave me depleted, and the only conclusion I can reach is that there are no winners in this case, only losers. Anyway, what's the point of agonizing if I'm not going to do anything about it? I'm locked inside myself. Is it time for me to break out? To give up? Days go by, weeks…. Time doesn't care about my feelings or my pain, it travels at its own pace, day after day, morning after night after morning. A bird chirps on my windowsill, reminding me that there is life outside my four walls. How will I break down all the barriers that I have built for myself? Will I walk out the door, go down to the street, lose myself in the sea of people walking this way and that? Will I pick up the phone and call? And who would I call? My friend Tamari, whom- along with the rest of the world- I've renounced? Even my brothers gave up, after I kept refusing to see them. Is it time to go back into their lives? Would they be willing to accept me? Is that what I really want? I have no idea.

When I got to Israel, by myself, my brothers were waiting for me, defending my husband, ordering me back to him and the children.

It never occurred to them that perhaps I was doing the right thing. Sometimes I even think they've convinced themselves that I did go back. That the reason they never speak to me or see me is that I've gone on a long trip with my family. Or maybe they think that if they showed any sign of support, I would never go back to my husband. In the beginning, they understood how hard it was for me in America, how much I longed to return to Israel. But, they said, my husband Dan loved me with all his soul, and when that kind of love comes your way, you don't let it slip away. Not to mention how terrible, how unforgiveable, it is for a mother to abandon her children, to sacrifice them just so she could live in Israel. My first responsibility was towards my husband and children. They didn't understand, they said in one voice, how I could turn my back on them and live alone in an apartment in Tel Aviv.

ΦΦΦ

To this day, I have only fond memories of working the land with my Garin. It was a magical time, in which anything was possible. The air itself was charged with electricity: there were no obstacles we couldn't surmount. Once our work was done and our rooms tidied up, we were free to do whatever we wanted. We had a lot of time on our hands, raging hormones, and plenty of opportunities to make our secret dreams come true. Between the desert heat and the mountains that surrounded us, we felt like we were all alone. It was blissful and liberating, and that's where D'vir and I consummated our love.

This period went by in a flash. Afterwards, the boys went up to Lebanon, and we were sent to farm a stretch of land far away from them. D'vir and I rarely saw each other, but our love continued to blossom. Perhaps it was because there was so much distance between us. Imagination outshone reality: we could yearn for each other, write each other love letters. I remember those days as one long stretch of yearning, which ended when we were reunited on kibbutz for the last stage of our army service, half a year of being together.

Slowly, over time, I began to think that perhaps what I had with D'vir wasn't the real thing. We had lots of fights, about nothing and everything, followed by passionate reconciliations. On the weekends, we'd hike through the desert with backpacks and a small tent; occasionally, we'd visit our parents. Then something terrible and unexpected happened, something that changed my life forever. My father died suddenly, and I returned home.

I will never forget that day. My father died in his sleep, so I never had a chance to tell him how much I loved him, to hug him, to say a real goodbye. One minute he was there, and then he disappeared from our lives, just like that. I was traumatized for a long time. I couldn't fall asleep at night because I was afraid I might not wake up. Was it in my genes? Had he passed it on, not just to me but to my brothers as well? I couldn't shake the fear, and the pain and longing were seared into my bones.

In the beginning, my mother was very practical. She worked during the day, and at night, she organized all the documents. Even with her job, she couldn't make enough to support us, so we had to sell our apartment and move to a smaller one. When we first talked about moving, I was the one who objected the most, but in the end, I was surprised to discover that the move actually helped me. I could finally stop searching for my father in every room. Of course, we brought all kinds of mementos with us-photographs, my father's glasses, his collection of antique stamps-but the walls smelled different, and they breathed new energy into our lives that had been so drastically transformed.

Around that time, I started working as a waitress. D'vir was still in the army, and when he'd come home on leave I was too exhausted to go anywhere, and anyway, I wasn't in the mood. When he completed his service, we looked for an apartment. We had always been planning, to live together, but I quickly realized that that would have been a mistake. Moreover, I had turned into an adult, albeit for sad reasons, and he was still a kid. His dream was to sleep all day and party all night. When I found myself taking care of him, as if he were a baby, I broke up with him. We never had a chance to live together. Then I moved to Haifa and enrolled in university.

August 22, 1991

Seattle

My dearest Tamari,

It feels strange to be writing to you again, after almost eight years. So much has happened to both of us over the years; so many things have changed. I'm a mother now, and you're about to become one…. We're both in stable relationships (or as stable as possible), we both went to school, learned a lot, had all kinds of experiences, some together, some apart…. It's nice to be writing each other again. I feel so close to you, almost as if you were sitting right next to me and the two of us were chatting away like we used to.

We reached this foreign land ten days ago. Dan started a new job, and Yonatan and I are busy exploring our new city, setting up our temporary house, and most of all, getting over jet lag. Yonatan starts his day at around three in the morning. He throws his pacifier on the floor and screams, "Cereal, Mommy, cereal!" We do our best to ignore his demands, hoping he'll tire himself out and fall back asleep, but it doesn't seem to be working. I try to let Dan sleep, since he's the one who has to get up and go to work in the morning. Needless to say, I can only hold out for a couple of minutes before I drag myself into the kitchen, pour some cereal for Yonatan, and sit with him in the living room, trying to steal a few more minutes of sleep. When he's done eating, he tosses his bowl in the air and shouts, "I get up, Mommy, I want get up!" How can I possibly hear a sentence like that and not scoop him up in my arms and snuggle with him and inhale the smell of shampoo on his hair and stroke his sweet body, even if it is the middle of the night and I'm a wreck and all I want to do is sleep…. After Yonatan pulls my nose, my eyelashes (maybe that will make me open my eyes!) and my hair, I read him a story, and we start our day. By the time Dan wakes up at 7:30, Yonatan's already taking his "afternoon nap." When he wakes up, we go for a stroll around the neighborhood.

The Israelis I've met here tell me that the best way to shake jet lag is to spend as much time as possible outside, and so Yonatan and I go for long walks. We explore a new area every day, and we've gotten to know the area quite well.

We live in a pleasant, quiet part of town, not far from a nice little lake that we visit almost daily. I pack snacks and a water bottle, and when we're tired of walking, we head to the lake. As we get closer, he starts shouting, "Water! Water!" When we get there, he runs over and dips his toes in the water. Then he shrieks, "I'm cold! I'm cold!" Same exact thing, day in and day out. Yonatan has his rituals. He sits in the shallow water and plays with his pail and shovel. Sometimes, if there are other kids around, they come over and try to play with us. Yonatan is thrilled, and I, too, am delighted. What a sweet and tiny bundle of joy he is! How he loves life! We play in the sand for a while, eat some fruit, and go back home. We've discovered a little playground, and even a small swimming pool, but I like the lake best of all.

The people here are very friendly. They say good morning when they pass me on the street, they ask us how we're doing, they tousle Yonatan's hair, they comment on his cuteness. The pace of life here is very foreign to me. Everything is calm; cars stop at the crosswalks, the drivers give you the right of way, nobody pushes... you get the sense that nobody here is in a rush. At the supermarket, people wait in line patiently, and the cashier asks how your day is going. What can I say, I like all this serenity. I find it soothing. It's like a little Garden of Eden in this crazy world of ours….

Seattle's very pretty, but it's strange to think that we're going to be here for a few solid years. It's not like we're on vacation or here temporarily; this place is going to be a home for me, maybe not "the home", but still. I'm told that summers here are very short, and that it's always raining, even in the summer. This past week, however, has been beautiful, so it's hard to believe what I hear. But if everyone's saying it, there must be some truth to it, right? I'm enclosing some photos: one of our neighborhood, one of Yonatan sitting on the porch, and one of the lake. See that enormous tree behind Yonatan? They're everywhere. I saw a woodpecker on one of the trees near our house- a good reminder that there is life outside of my four walls. Right now, we're still in our temporary house. We'll have to start looking for a place to rent or buy, but we still haven't decided exactly what we're looking for.

Kisses to everyone. I hope you have a chance to visit my mother. Let me know what's going on in your life, and how your pregnancy is going.

Regards to Doron,

Love,

Me!

September 6, 1991

Tel Aviv

Hey Michalush,

I was so happy to get your first letter. I'm keeping it in a box with all the other letters you've written to me over the years. I found myself re-reading some of them, and I can't believe how much our lives have changed. After that horrible period I went through in high school, I would never have believed that I'd be able to trust a man. Or that I'd get pregnant! The whole idea used to terrify me, but with Doron, it's different. I feel so safe, so loved....

I still can't believe I'm about to become a mother, and I can't stop thinking about what kind of mother I will be. Whenever I see a baby on the street, I wonder how the mothers can tolerate all that crying.... Then I push that thought out of my head and keep on walking. There's no point in agonizing over it. Doron is thrilled at the prospect of becoming a father, but I'm petrified. How will I be able to love this tiny creature? These thoughts keep me up at night. At least I know that even if I can't love this little person growing inside me, Doron can. That's how he is: when he loves someone, he loves them with all his heart. I think he's going to be a fabulous father.

Overall, the pregnancy is progressing well. It's been 28 weeks already: 12 more to go until zero hour. The truth is, this little being (we've resisted the temptation to find out the baby's sex) has taken over my entire life. It rules my soul. If this tiny creature can keep me up at night, with all its kicking and wiggling around, it must be in excellent shape. Just like its mother! (Actually, it's not just the kicking that keeps me up- it's also the thoughts racing through my head….)

My mother is so excited about having a grandchild, she's making me crazy. She calls me ten times a day to make sure I'm eating and drinking and resting, and she disapproves of my wild lifestyle. Ever since my sister came out as a lesbian, my parents don't expect much from her anymore. They're still struggling to come to terms with it, even though she's already announced her plans to move in with her girlfriend, Orit. My sister doesn't seem the least bit maternal, and even if she did, it would be a strange and complicated kind of motherhood, even for my parents,

funny how things turn out. She was their pride and joy, the success story, and I was the troublemaker; now we've switched roles, and I'm the one they're boasting about. Granted, their approval is limited- after all, Doron and I aren't married, they don't like the thought of us living together, and they almost fainted when they found out I was pregnant- but it's approval nonetheless. They've been dying for grandchildren. As you know, I'm not about to change my lifestyle just to meet their expectations. My father is still so ashamed of me, he can hardly look me in the eye, but he'll get used to it.

It's been very hot all week, and humid, too, which is a nightmare. We try to go to the beach in the evenings. The further along I get in the pregnancy, the harder it is for me to cope with the heat. I'm a nervous wreck, and poor Doron keeps trying to come up with creative ways to calm me down. Work is fine, still crazy, as always.

Working in public relations is intense and demanding, but I love every minute of it. I never thought I'd find a career that I loved so much, and now it's been three years and I'm still not tired of it.

I'm glad to hear that you're living somewhere pretty and peaceful. Knowing myself, five minutes of that kind of peacefulness would be enough to drive me mad. I need noise and chaos; I need to work hard and play hard.

Sweetie, I miss you so much, now more than ever. I hope that we can visit you in the beautiful place you're living in. I also hope that you can be here when the baby is born, just as you promised.

P.S. I spoke to your mother on the phone this week; she sounds fine. She told me that she and her friend took a little trip up north and that she's hardly ever home. I can understand that. After all, since your father died, she's the only breadwinner. I think your brothers are OK, too. They're both in school, right?

Your mother said you called her and told her that Seattle is amazing. She misses Yonatan terribly, and she's already planning her visit.

2005

We were already married when we left Israel, and our son was almost two. Dan was working full-time; I was working more than full-time. Life was just an endless, crazy race against time. Yonatan was always sick, Dan kept being called up for reserve duty, and I was under constant stress. I didn't like living in this pressure cooker, and I really wanted another child, a daughter, to be exact.

We started to think about moving to the United States for several reasons, including our financial situation that brought us to the conclusion that as long as we are in Israel we won`t be able to afford a second child. e of which was the security situation. Every time I drove somewhere in my car, with my son sitting in the back seat, I would found myself trying to stay away from the busses, in case they blew up. I avoided public places as best as I could. I was feeling increasingly stifled, to the point where I was hardly feeling safe outside of our apartment. If we left for a few years, Dan said, we'd be able to have another baby, to travel, to get away from all the economic stress, to see the world. It would only be temporary. It was a difficult decision to make, primarily because of my mother and my brothers. I didn't want them to feel hurt.

In the end, we decide to go to Washington State, and we settled in a suburb of Seattle, near the Microsoft campus. Dan immediately took a job at Microsoft, and I started looking into childcare. There was an opening for Yonatan at the local JCC. To my delight, everything seemed to be falling into place.

Yonatan cried every day for a month. This highly verbal child, who used to sing Hebrew songs all the time, who knew how to express himself so beautifully, was floundering in this new language. Until an Israeli teacher began working in his classroom, he couldn't find his place.

Little by little, we got used to it. We bought an old house and immediately started renovations, some by ourselves, some with professional help. Dan turned out to be a real handy-man: he tended the garden, spruced up the kitchen, fixed whatever needed fixing. As for me, I had lots of time on my hands. I redecorated our cozy little nest, finished all the work for my master's, taught some Hebrew, and, above all, yearned for Israel.

The neighborhood we lived in was full of virgin forests, verdant meadows, lakes and streams. We spent our first few years hiking and exploring; back then, I was sure that our time in this lovely place was limited. For many years, I was filled with a sense of transience. What changed was my world view. In the end, wasn't everything transient? Including us? There was no point in tormenting myself with thoughts of "What if we hadn't left Israel?" Everyone who leaves their homeland, even for a few years, always wonders what would have happened if they had never left.

I tried to think of myself as a turtle carrying its house on its back. Home wasn't the walls of my house, or the town I lived in; it was my husband and children. Yes, walls and towns matter, too, but in the final analysis, the people I am with are my home.

I remember the first time this thought popped into my head. Dan had flown to Israel for work, and I felt lost without him. I couldn't understand how a few hours earlier- when he was still here- I felt at home, and now, everything seemed completely foreign.

Whenever he was away, my house felt foreign to me; then he'd come back and it would feel like home again. That's when I realized that Dan would always be my home, whether we lived in a tent or a palace.

The difference between life in Israel and life in America was enormous. I was pleasantly surprised by the pace of life, the politeness, the calm way people drove, the way people waited in line instead of trying to cut in front of you. I loved these things from the start. Americans respect the law, for better and for worse (and sometimes to the point of absurdity). It was reassuring to know that people weren't always out to take advantage of you. Everyone smiled; drivers let you into their lanes, and didn't honk the second the light changed. I could feel my blood pressure getting lower by the minute.

But what really won me over was the respect people felt towards motherhood. Whenever I went somewhere with my small children, people commented on how hard it is to be a mother, how much self-sacrifice it required, and how my kids looked so happy. This sympathetic approach to motherhood alleviated some of the pressure I'd been feeling to find self-fulfillment in my career. Here, being a mother was the most important job a person could have. I committed myself to motherhood with every fiber of my being, happily relinquishing all my other dreams to do so. Of course, little by little, I found myself sinking into bitterness. There was more to me, it turned out, than motherhood.

September 22, 1991

Seattle

Tamari,

This is the first time in my entire life that I'm not with my family for the holidays. During Rosh Hashanah and Yom Kippur, there is no sense of festivity or solemnity on the streets of Seattle.

Fortunately, we met Yael and Yoel, a lovely Israeli couple, more or less our age. Their little girl, Maya, is a bit older than Yonatan. They came here three months ago, and we connected immediately. Yael is very sweet. She grew up in Jerusalem, served as an officer in the army's education department, and studied psychology in college. Yoel works for a small high-tech company that brought him in from Israel. Anyway, their background is very similar to ours, and we enjoy being together. We had dinner with them on Rosh Hashanah, and we even went to synagogue on Yom Kippur. Even so, there was no holiday spirit in the air, and it made me a little sad. Dan tried to cheer me up, reminding me that we'd only just arrived, and that we had to give it a chance. Next year, my mother will be able to spend the holidays with us.

The holidays were tough for my mother, with us being so far away. She didn't say anything; on the contrary, she kept saying how nice it was to spend the holidays with my aunt. But I could hear the sadness in her voice. She didn't want me to feel bad, but I know that spending the holiday without my father and without us couldn't have been easy. It's true; my brothers were there, but still.

I've started looking around for good childcare, and we've found a nice house for sale. Don't worry, we're not planning to stay here for the rest of our lives, but buying a house makes economic sense. I've already looked at five daycare centers, all different. It seems that there are all kinds of educational approaches, and many options to choose from. In every single school I visited, I felt utterly out of place. What do I care about the Montessori Method, or any other method, if they don't celebrate the Jewish holidays or welcome the Shabbat? Can you believe I'm writing this? I feel like I'm in the middle of some sort of religious crisis. On the one hand, I'm completely secular, but at the same time, I'm searching for my Jewish identity. It's crazy. I heard there's a Jewish kindergarten not too far away, but it's not that close, either: half an hour's drive each way. Still, I'll check it out in the near future.

I think you're right- you really would hate it here! It's true, nothing ever happens, and that's exactly what I like about it!

I miss you so much. How's your pregnancy going? Try to take it easy, and to appreciate all the beauty in your life. After all, you have a terrific boyfriend, and before you know it, you'll be a mother.

Write soon and often,

Michal

2005

Whenever I took my children to the Jewish Community Center, I made a point of driving up a steep road that reminded me, albeit fleetingly, of "Derech HaYam," the main thoroughfare leading up to Haifa's Mount Carmel. Like Derech HaYam, this road was lined with pine trees, and the houses that peeked out from behind a bend in the road looked just like the ones we passed on the way to Mount Carmel. Every time we took that road, I would- for a few seconds- feel completely at home, and, at the same time, heartbroken. My Yonatan was born in Haifa, and we used to drive up the Sea Road every week, on our way home from visiting our parents. Sometimes we'd stop to say hello to my cousins, who lived nearby. My instinct to look for "the house" wherever I went had been passed down to my children. Sometimes I would hear them talking in the back seat. "Wow, this really reminds me of Grandma's street...." When we lived in Israel, I never searched for other countries. Israel is my heart, it is my soul, despite all the complicated feelings it elicits. It seems to me now that back then, I was consumed with longing for the land that I loved; now I am consumed with longing for my children.

Time has become meaningless. Every day is like all the others, and there is no distinction between weekdays and Shabbat and holidays. Having a routine comforts me, and anyway, what is there for me to look forward to? Routine preserves what little sanity I still have. It helps me cope with my endless longing for my children; it distracts me from my life, and from where my life is going: the sun rises and sets the voices from outside my apartment change as the hours pass. But it is my routine, and it protects me. It's been a few days since I've seen Roni. Maybe he's been called up for reserve duty? Iris, I've noticed, has been coming home at her usual time, so I know everything is OK and I can go to sleep. When I lie down in bed, I look at the pictures of my children, and in my mind, I can feel their warm, soft necks. Their absence is excruciating, and sometimes I ask myself what I was thinking when I left everything and came here. I forgive them for all the hardships they heaped upon me, but I cannot forgive their father for his lies.

When my children got older and no longer needed me the way they used to, I had a hard time. It wasn't simply that they didn't need me- they tried to pretend I didn't even exist. Maybe they saw me as used and tattered, something they could crumple up whenever they wanted to, something they were free to trample on.

When Yonatan started first grade, he was diagnosed with a learning disability. I sat with him for hours, helping him with his homework. Yonatan struggled, and it pained me to watch him suffer. Throughout all his school years, I helped him with everything, until he decided that my English wasn't good enough, and that my knowledge of science was, in his words, "ridiculously limited." He didn't want my help anymore. That's when we started drifting apart. The solution to his problems, he decided, was Dan, and he never turned to me again. Gradually, he stopped sharing other aspects of his life with me, too, and I felt like I had become a burden. I took comfort in the knowledge that Abigail still needed me, but of course her time came, too, and at an even younger age than her brother. Perhaps she was trying to follow in his footsteps. Little by little, I felt like I had lost my place in my own family.

October 9, 1991

Tel Aviv

Hey Michali,

I've been lying in bed for more than a week now, after spending five days in the hospital. I'm on bed rest, and it's a nightmare. It started when I felt a little pressure in my lower abdomen, but I figured it was normal. (What do I know, I've never been pregnant before...) Then one day, I wasn't feeling well, so I left work early. By the time I got home, the pressure had turned into pain. Doron was at a meeting in Haifa, but my mother came immediately. I tried to rest, but I couldn't fall asleep. Doron was on his way home, and I heard him arguing with my mother on the phone. She was saying that I had to get to the hospital right away, and he was telling her that she was being hysterical. By the end of the conversation, they were both shouting.

When he got home, we decided that I had to go to the hospital, and throughout the entire drive, the two of them fought over who was right and when they should have headed towards the hospital, and I was so anxious that I thought I was going to give birth right there in the car, so I screamed as loud as I could for them to shut up before I kicked them out of the car and drove myself to the hospital, and that seemed to quiet them down. As soon as we got to the hospital, two nurses jumped on me and alerted the doctor, who told me that I was about to give birth but maybe they could stop labor. The pressure I felt, it turned out, was contractions, and if they couldn't stop the labor from progressing, I would give birth at thirty-five weeks, which isn't terrible but isn't good, either. While they filled me up with drugs, all these people came up and touched me and inspected me, as if I were an old battered car. In the end they managed to stabilize me. They kept me there, pumped full of drugs that made me shiver constantly, night and day- it was awful. I want this to be over already! This is the last time I'm ever getting pregnant. Make sure I remember that, OK?

Time doesn't pass, the days don't go by. I used to be so active, but I've turned into a couch potato. Yesterday I made Doron take me out of the house, and we returned to find two hysterical mothers, wondering where we'd disappeared to. They were positive I had gone to the hospital, and they were about to drive over to check. Of course, I got an earful about how irresponsible I was, and Doron got a lecture about how he always gave in to me. They berated me for always doing whatever I want whether or not it made sense. What will happen to the child, it's not good for it to be born so prematurely, etc.

It's driving me nuts, this obsession with the baby. Nobody's seen it, nobody knows it, it can't do anything on its own, and yet that's all anyone ever talks about. As for me, I seem to be nothing more than a truck carrying precious cargo, or the peel of a very rare fruit. Nobody cares about how much pain I'm in. Nobody asks me how it feels to blow up like a balloon, or to have someone kick you relentlessly from the inside, or to shiver constantly. Where am I in this picture? And what will happen after the baby is born? Will I even exist? Can I go back in time? Is it too late to change my mind?

It kills me that you're not here. I know you would come over and calm me down and entertain me. Maybe the two of us could even escape to a café somewhere and forget about the rest of the world. And to answer your question: no, we haven't prepared ourselves for the birth. Where's the fire?

When are you coming already? And how are Yonatan and Dan?

Tamar

ϕϕϕ

Both her life with Doron and her pregnancy struck me as miraculous. When I saw that she had managed to build a new life for herself, with someone so level-headed and stable, someone who loved her fiercely, my heart filled with joy.

The years, right after our army service, flew by. We both went to school- she studied product management, and I studied occupational therapy. While she was in school she met Doron and moved in with him, despite the objections of his parents who insisted that she was "too bohemian, too unstable, and simply not good enough" for their perfect son. Once they realized how much their son loved Tamari, they put their reservations aside and welcomed her into the family.

I was the first person she told about her pregnancy, and I promised to fly in for the delivery (unfortunately, I couldn't keep my word). All women feel like pregnancy is endless, but for Tamari, the time passed excruciatingly slowly. She felt like an alien being was taking over her body, and she couldn't wait for that feeling to go away. She was terrified of becoming a mother, and by the time she acknowledged that, it was too late. It's not that I think she wanted to terminate the pregnancy; it's just that she was scared of this little creature that was entirely dependent on her. I can sympathize with that feeling: my life, too, was changed forever with the birth of my oldest son. The difference is that I had been waiting for that change my whole life. When it was time for her to give birth, and I realized I couldn't be there with her, I felt awful.

We spoke on the phone when her contractions first began, and we spoke again right after the baby was born, when she was flooded with emotion. I suppose that in a way, I was with her during this miracle, even if it was from a distance.

When I was studying occupational therapy at Haifa University- in my last years in Israel- I loved school so much that all I wanted was to take classes for the rest of my life. In order to pay my tuition, I had to work as a substitute teacher, a waitress, and even a house cleaner, but I felt as free as a bird. I didn't depend on anyone, only late at night would I fantasize about meeting the love of my life.

One day, when I went out to a movie with some friends, a computer science student from the Technion came along. He was quiet, diligent, and utterly humorless... and that's what made me fall in love with him. Looking back, I realize that I fell in love with him because he was so different than D'vir. D'vir- who walked around wearing Indian shirts, never cut his hair, played guitar on the streets, and didn't have a shred of responsibility or maturity. And he had no desire to study. Dan, on the other hand, studied hard, supported himself, and lived in the dorms- or more accurately, in the library. His assiduousness and quiet demeanor won me over. I felt like I could depend on him, I could lean on him, and from that perspective, he never let me down. For many years I believed that he was the love of my life, and I followed him wherever he went. I made a home with him and had children with him- until everything fell apart.

Over the years, we drifted apart, him and me, and each of us burrowed into our own worlds. I was pained by the growing distance between us (at least until I found out the truth). I immersed myself in my children's world, and cut myself off from the outside world, and from him. My children's closeness and neediness filled my life, and I wanted nothing more than having them near me. But in the end, even they abandoned me.

I haven't seen D'vir for many years. I was shocked to hear, from mutual friends, that he had cut his hair, stopped playing street music, and- most surprising of all- gone back to school. They told me he had gotten married and had a daughter; beyond that, I knew nothing.

November 15, 1991

Tel Aviv

Hi Michali,

Thank you for the flowers, and for your warm wishes. Lianne is fine, and I'm doing much better. The C-section was the last thing I wanted, but all that craziness is behind me. Now I'm in the middle of a different kind of craziness. My mother comes every morning and stays until Doron comes home from work. She tries her best to help me, but I don't really have the energy to deal with her. She spends the whole day trying to convince me to nurse Lianne! My boobs are killing me, I'm exhausted, and all I want is for everyone to leave me alone and let me sleep. Is that so much to ask? Am I being unreasonable? Does the future of the entire world depend upon a pair of painful and tired breasts? When my mother leaves and Doron finally comes home, I present him with Lianne, and his whole face lights up. He talks to her as if she's already sixteen. "Tell Daddy about your day, darling. Did you work hard? What life lessons did you learn?" He tells her how much he loves her, and how her mother is the most amazing woman because she brought her into the world and made Doron a father. Then he comes over and kisses me, and sometimes he even makes me smile. This touching and entertaining performance has been re-enacted every night since we got home from the hospital.

I try not to think about all the things that bothered me before the birth. I made a resolution to start each day with a clean slate. Lianne is incredibly sweet, but I can't honestly say that I've gotten used to having her around, or that I fell in love with her the minute I saw her. Sure, I feel responsible for her, I care about her, but nonetheless she's a major annoyance. (How can such a tiny body make so much noise?) I'm mixed up, my whole life has been turned upside-down, there's no day and no night, everything revolves around Lianne, and it wipes me out.

I miss you so much. I know that if you were here, you'd be able to cheer me up, or you'd kick my mother out of the house and give Lianne a bottle and take some of the pressure off me. I have to go now- she's crying. Write and tell me what you've been up to. I can't wait to see you. When are you coming?

Here's a photo from the hospital, and another one from our bedroom, where the little peanut sleeps next to our bed.

Hugs and kisses,

Tamari

ϕϕϕ

Motherhood is such a big word. Whenever I try to talk about my own experience as a mother, I am flooded with mixed emotions. For a long time, motherhood was all I ever wanted. It promised self-fulfillment, a sense of belonging, an outlet for all the love inside me, a stronger connection with my husband. It was my biggest dream: even when I was very young, I was ready for motherhood. I wanted a child of my own, someone I could love unconditionally, someone who would love me back, who was truly mine.

My pregnancy with our first son was relatively short: 36 weeks, including five weeks of bed rest in which I barely moved. Two of those weeks were spent in the hospital in Haifa. I didn't even get to see my son- whom I had been waiting for all my life- until ten hours after his birth. He was in the NICU, and I had just had surgery, so we couldn't meet right away. I begged and pleaded, and when they finally brought him to me, I looked into the glass case where he was lying on his belly, and like magic, he opened his eyes and looked at me. The next few minutes were miraculous. I stared at this tiny baby, who weighed less than five pounds, who was practically skin and bones, who looked a little like a shriveled old man, and I couldn't comprehend how I had been able to bring such a magnificent creature into the world. How could I have given birth to such a beautiful little boy?

When I left the hospital a few days later, I went home without him. Think about it: a young mother recovering from surgery, who herself is in need of care and healing, has to go home without her baby. It was terribly traumatic. Five days after the operation, I had to drive an old stick-shift to the hospital if I wanted to see my son. Every time I stepped on the clutch, I was in agony. I tried to breastfeed him, but it was a lost cause: he simply didn't have the strength. I stubbornly pumped milk for a while, but in the end I gave up.

I'm trying to understand why society pressures women to breastfeed. It's nothing short of abusive, crushing young mothers like a steamroller. Who has the right to tell a woman what to do with her body? Do you become transparent the minute you start to carry a child in your womb? Who has the right to bully another woman, to tell her not to give up, to hang in there, that it's all for the good of the baby? Why aren't we more sympathetic towards these "human incubators" that not only have to carry the fetus, but have to nurse it, too?

Motherhood is incredibly demanding, but it is also very beautiful. I don't hold much stock with "love at first sight." I don't think that a maternal instinct washes over you the instant the baby is born, and stays with you for life. It's true, the thought that this child was mine, really mine, that nobody could take him away from me, was so strong it almost hurt. The idea that I would be with him forever, that this miniscule creature was completely dependent on me, that I would always give him everything is, on the other hand, a scary thought. Giving birth left me in a state of shock. I had been waiting so eagerly for the moment I could hold my child, but when he was born, there was sadness mingled in with the joy: my body, that had grown so accustomed to taking this creature with me wherever I went, sometimes happily, sometimes reluctantly, was suddenly empty. It didn't have a chance to adjust to this new situation. When my body was suddenly infused with silence, when I no longer felt his every movement, I knew that from now on we were two separate beings. That was almost too hard to bear. I couldn't understand why I was so sad; after all, it was this very separation that gave my body back to me. The stillness was agonizing, and at the same time, liberating. Along with the pain of separation came a distinct feeling of relief.

The birth of my son radically transformed our family. I belonged completely to Yonatan. He was the bible that I pored over, day and night. I tried to understand him from every possible angle, and I tried to anticipate his every need before he had a chance to show his displeasure. I cared for my newborn baby as if he were the very essence of me, something I had been missing all my life. In the first few months after the birth, Dan didn't complain, but as time went by, I could see him pulling away from his son. I hadn't seen this coming. Yes, he changed his diapers and bathed him, but he seemed to be doing so mechanically, without any emotion. He wanted to hold me in his arms, to be the only person in my life. Of course that never happened.

The beginning of motherhood was one of the hardest periods of my life, but only now can I admit it. I couldn't figure out how to transform myself from a woman into a mother, or how my body was supposed to manage this dual role. For a long time after the birth, I felt no sexual desire whatsoever, despite Dan's best efforts. He did everything he could, including looking after the baby, to bring me around. It wasn't easy. I was exhausted both night and day, and sex was the last thing I wanted; Dan couldn't forgive me for that. My difficulties with breastfeeding, my changed body, and the pressure of being both a wife and a mother, closed up any doors between my heart and his. I didn't have any patience for his wants and needs, and he felt neglected. At one point he even stopped talking to me, which only made me angrier and more defensive. One day he finally exploded. He was tired of being a household appliance, whose only purpose was to make my life easier. Unless something changed, he said, he was going to pack his bags and go somewhere where he was treated like a human being.

These words burned inside me, stabbing my heart like knives. I felt sadness and revulsion and pity, and- most of all- fear. Bemoaning my inability to be a real wife to him, I, too, fell apart. I took out all my pain and heartache on him. In the end, we reconciled, and were closer than ever.

January 5, 1992

Tel Aviv

Michali,

What would I do without you? Your letter arrived three days ago, and it made me feel so free. It was as if all the air that had been trapped in my throat came rushing out. I told Doron that I'd had enough, to hell with nursing, Lianne would survive without it, and we switched to a bottle. The biggest advantage of bottle-feeding is that now Doron can take her in the middle of the night, and I can finally get some sleep.

Your letter has become my mantra. You made me realize that I have to stop stressing out so much. I have to just sit back and let things flow. I always thought your connection with Yonatan came naturally; I saw you as a kind of "earth mother." So if you tell me that it won't be the end of the world if I don't nurse, it must be true. You're right, I really hated it. My nipples were always sore, my boobs were always showing… I was trying so hard to please everyone else. I couldn't bring myself to acknowledge that this just wasn't me! Who was I kidding?

The first time I gave Lianne a bottle, I discovered- to my astonishment- that she wasn't all that keen on breastfeeding, either. She chugged down the formula in five minutes, then fell asleep for three hours. I had to check on her to make sure she was still breathing! Before I started giving her formula, she would wake up every hour and a half or so. In between naps, I'd be burping her and changing her diaper. Day and night, it was the same continuous, exhausting cycle: eat, poop, eat, poop.

It's been three days, and I feel like a different person. I'm less tired than I was, and my stitches are starting to heal. We go for walks every day, unless it's raining or very cold. We stroll through the streets of Tel Aviv, stopping to rest in the park every now and then. Sometimes I bring a book, but mostly I sit and watch the people go by, or chat with the other moms. It's nice. Did you know there's such a thing as "The Sisterhood of Mothers?" Really! Mothers pushing strollers like to sit next to each other and schmooze about their babies, and about themselves, and they almost always "click." We can talk about anything, because we all have the same problems; we just have different ways of dealing with them. I've been thinking that "when I grow up," I want to take a video camera to the park and interview these women about their lives. I think it would make a great movie. Is there a sisterhood like this in Seattle? I imagine that it would feel strange, forming close friendships in any language other than Hebrew. Am I right?

Aside from all that, everything's fine. I don't need a thing, other than you!

I miss you so much, and I'm counting the days until your visit,

Tamari

February 2, 1992

Hi Tamari,

I'm glad I was able to help. Considering the distance and the time difference between us, that's about all I can do. Overall, everything is fine, but it rains all the time, and I miss Israel so much. I'm so anxious to get back to the Holy Land; I'm ready to kiss the ground….

You asked if there's a "Sisterhood of Mothers," and the answer is yes, there is, but it's different from the one in Israel. Here, it's easy for me to meet other moms, and to connect with them instantly, but the conversations are shallow. Something along the lines of, "What's new? What an adorable little boy. Where'd you get his shirt, at the Gap? There's an amazing sale at whatever store," etc. I suppose it's just a different culture here.

Lately, quite a few families have been moving here from Israel. I've managed to meet most of them, and as a result, our social life is taking off. We meet for coffee at Starbucks, we have Shabbat dinner together. It's like our own little kibbutz, which gives me a sense of belonging. Of course, it's nothing compared to being at home.

I spoke to my mother a couple of days ago. She's been sick all week, and my brothers have been taking care of her (luckily, they're good guys), but even so, I felt very guilty. I'm not there for her, and that's not right. When I said this to Dan, he asked me why I always have to focus on what I don't have instead on what I do have. After all, my brothers were able to take care of her, so it all ended well. Who said it has to be me taking care of her all the time? I found his response disappointing. What kind of mindset is that? My mother raised me, and she lost her husband, and now she's losing me, too? I had hoped that Dan would understand me, but all he can think about is work. He feels like he has to prove himself, so he's working non-stop. I didn't respond to him, and I decided that from now on, I'm not going to say another word about my life here and the toll it's taking on me. All things considered, I have a good life, and I have nothing to complain about. Dan's earning a nice salary, and he tries to help out around the house. On the weekends, he takes Yonatan to the museum or the park so I can have a little break, and from time to time, he even tries his hand at cooking.

Life here is pleasant and serene, and the people are friendly and polite. Maybe these are just growing pains; after all, we've only been here for six months. In any case, we're spending this weekend in Vancouver, a city in Canada. I'll let you know how it goes.

Love you and miss you,

Michal

ΦΦΦ

She missed me terribly after the baby was born. She could barely function. All the pressure- to be a mother and a wife, to keep house, to work, to be a good daughter- paralyzed her. She felt like she was letting everyone down. She and I were in constant contact, and I tried to support her from a distance. I did my best to raise her spirits, and I was there for her whenever she needed me, day or night.

She'd had a difficult pregnancy, and she couldn't identify with the sense of completeness I felt during pregnancy, and the sense of emptiness I felt after Yonatan was born. She hated the feeling of having another person living in her body, doing as he pleased, and she couldn't wait for that little intruder to go out into the world and leave her in peace. She wasn't at all prepared for what happened after the birth: the sleep deprivation, the fatigue. Caring for a helpless little creature left her utterly depleted. She waited for that moment of liberation, when she would be freed from all her distress; when it finally hit her that the moment she was waiting for would never arrive, she fell apart.

And I, who had always been there for her, was far away. I couldn't hold her in my arms, I couldn't take care of her; I could only help her from a distance, and it broke my heart. I promised her I'd visit as soon as I could, but I knew that wouldn't be for a long time, especially since I had a small child of my own who needed me.

When she stopped nursing, on my recommendation, things got a bit better. Her family rallied around her, and little by little, she improved. Spring arrived, and she started walking with the baby through the streets of Tel Aviv. The rainy days were the worst, when the two of them had to stay indoors. She felt smothered, and she hated it.

She wrote that she liked being a mother, but I wondered if she genuinely enjoyed her new life, or if she just liked the appellation. I suspected she wasn't being completely honest with herself. She was always complaining about exhaustion, and she claimed that Lianne was a particularly difficult child who wouldn't give her a moment's peace. For Tamari, every night was a losing battle.

The fact that she couldn't decipher all of Lianne's needs made Tamari crazy. She was frustrated, angry, and defeated. She couldn't wait to go back to work, to get dressed, to make herself pretty, to meet with other adults, to take care of "important" things instead of "pee-poop all day long." When the grandmothers agreed to take turns watching Lianne, saving Tamari from having to search for a nanny, she felt like a huge burden had been taken off her shoulders.

And she continued to wait for me. She wrote me long letters thanking me for all my support. She drafted a detailed itinerary for my visit, which was planned for the following Passover: we'd go back to the Sidney Alley Beach, we'd picnic in the Ben Shemen forest, we'd look for flowers. I, too, was counting on this trip to revive my spirit. I couldn't wait to set foot on the land of Israel. To feel, once again, like myself.

March 2, 1992

Seattle

Hey Sweetie,

I wanted to tell you all about our trip. Tamari, it was incredible! Vancouver is a beautiful, vibrant city, with lots of little shops (just like Israel), gorgeous architecture, a great farmer's market, and an endless sea. We brought our bicycles with us and went riding through Stanley Park, a giant park with a long bike trail. Dan pulled Yonatan behind him in a little cart, which we filled with toys and candy. I rode next to them, and I was so content. I felt so proud of my little family. At the same time, I felt a little sad that you weren't there. Vancouver reminded me so much of home, even though they're on opposite sides of the world. I suddenly found myself yearning for Israel. I've felt that sense of yearning many times before, but there, riding the bike, a gentle breeze blowing on my face, the pain was so acute I burst into tears. Dan and Yonatan didn't even notice, and I didn't particularly want to share my feelings with them. It was you I wanted, and you weren't there…. I wanted to be somewhere else, somewhere warmer. It's so cold and rainy here, and when I think about springtime in Israel, the fragrance in the air, all I want to do is go home. After the bike ride, we went to the city's beautiful aquarium, and I was able to push my sadness aside and enjoy myself. Yonatan was in seventh heaven! He loved the dolphins and the brightly colored fish, and Dan's explanations. I looked on from the side and thought about how lucky I am.

Here I am, going on and on about myself, and I haven't even asked how you are. I hope that bottle-feeding has made things easier for you, and that you're letting other people help you. I've started getting ready for our trip home- only two weeks and two days to go! I bought my mother a silk scarf from the outdoor market in Vancouver. I still haven't gotten anything for my brothers. I'm bringing all kinds of adorable little-girl things for Lianne: a pink dress, cute little socks, a hair ribbon, and an activity center, because "it's never too early to think about a child's education." I still haven't gotten anything for you; maybe I'll bring you a snow globe with a miniature "Space Needle" inside. (The Space Needle is the symbol of Seattle. It looks like a spaceship perched on a giant needle, and during the winter, it's covered with snow, so the snow globe will give you a taste of my life here.) What else? Maybe something to wear?

I hope there's a letter from you on its way, and that it arrives before I leave. I'm dreaming about the beach, I don't care which one…. And about the scent of flowers, and most of all about the hot, healing sun, to offset the chill of Washington.

Love,

Michal

ϕϕϕ

That first visit to Israel is etched in my memory forever. I felt joy
and wholeness and a fierce connection to the country. As our
plane started its descent, I looked down at my beloved land, and
everything I saw nearly brought me to tears. I kept asking myself
why I ever agreed to go to the United States. After all those hours
on the plane with Yonatan, Dan couldn't wait to land. He looked
wiped out. He never shows his feelings, and it occurred to me that
perhaps he was just looking forward to some rest. Dan had lost
interest in this little country long ago. Sure, he was glad to be on
vacation, and it would be nice to see his family, but from the
moment we arrived he started counting the days until our return.
Dan left Israel because he was tired of the day-to-day stress and
of being called up to the reserves all the time; he yearned for "a
normal, autonomous life, like every other normal person in the
western world." A life in which the country serves you instead of
the other way around. From the moment he left Israel, the move
had been a huge relief. The very things that were hardest for me,
like being away from close family, were, in Dan's eyes, ideal.
Nobody stuck their noses in his business, and he didn't feel
responsible for anyone's happiness, aside from his wife and child.
The idea of being a foreigner didn't bother him; weren't we
citizens of the world? We were all human, and it didn't matter
what country or culture you came from, as long as you were a
moral person. I asked him, more than once, what he meant by "a
moral person." Who was this moral person he kept talking about?
His answers were pragmatic: to him, a moral person was someone
who paid his taxes, obeyed the law, and donated money to

125

charity every now and then. That was the extent of his personal code of ethics, of his approach to life. He didn't question the morality of not keeping your promises. Was it moral to deceive your wife, year after year after year? Was it moral to keep her away from everything she dreamed about? Perhaps he didn't deceive me intentionally, but somewhere inside him he kept hoping that I would have a change of heart, that I would decide to make America my home. In my book, all of his empty promises to go back to Israel "in another year or two" constituted deception. His "year or two" lasted for fourteen years.

Dan was blessed with an equanimity that served him well, first in his career, then later on in amateur sports. Our family was a nice addition to his lifestyle, but as the years passed, I began to think that he would have been just fine without us, too. In fact, I wondered if we were more of a burden than anything else. Our "liberation" from Israel, which Dan thought of as a gift, was a formidable obstacle for me. I had never imagined raising my children anywhere but Israel, I never thought of my family as a burden, and in my eyes, reserve duty was an opportunity to serve the country that I so ardently loved.

From the moment we landed in Ben Gurion to the moment we departed, I walked around in a haze, as if I were drunk. I soaked up all the smells and basked in the warmth- of the people as well as the climate. I spent as much time as I could with my mother and my brothers, who were living at home while they were completing their studies. I visited Dan's family, too, and saw a few friends, but mostly I hung out with Tamari. And the more time we spent together, the more I realized how much we had in common. I was sure that we would be friends forever.

Now that Tamari had become a mother, we could finally share our thoughts on motherhood. Lianne was a sweet baby, happy and easy-going; almost as if she realized that her mother was having a hard time and needed special consideration. Tamari was doing much better, now that she was getting some sleep. She had gone back to work, and the change did her good. She was very committed to her job, and whenever she had to stay late, Doron would come home early and take care of the baby. It seemed to me that Tamari's life was back on track. I cherished every minute we spent together, the two of us with our little ones, as we wove a tapestry of happy moments and shared experiences.

May 8, 1992

Seattle

We came back here three days ago, and I've been in a funk ever since. The jetlag is even worse on the way back, probably because it's so rainy and gray here. Yonatan is, once again, up all night. I do my best to get him back to sleep without waking Dan, but it's hard. The return flight was unbearably long, and now, more than ever, I yearn to be back in Israel. How can Israelis stay here for so many years? I don't think I can spend the rest of my life in this country. Yes, it's very nice here, but it's sad, too, because in the end, it's just not my home, just a temporary replacement.

My Israeli friends tell me I'm suffering from "Returning-from-Israel Syndrome"; they laugh, and assure me that it won't last more than a week. Does everyone feel this way? How can they feel this way and still choose to live here for so many years? Personally, I am absolutely certain that I'm only here temporarily. Dan was thrilled to be back, and returned to work as soon as we got home, leaving me at home with all the rain, and with Yonatan who sleeps all day and is up all night. I have plenty of time to think, and what I think is that I want another child. I haven't mentioned this to Dan, but the fact is, Yonatan is getting bigger, and since I don't have a work permit, I'm home anyway, so it seems like the right time. What do you think? Yonatan will have a playmate, and I'm longing to hold a baby in my arms again. I think that Dan will like the idea: as long as I'm happy and he doesn't have to keep me entertained, Dan is content. Another alternative is that I get a job, but it can take years to get a permit. For now, I'm staying home.

I was so glad that you and I had a chance to "steal" a few hours to walk together through the streets of Tel Aviv, just the two of us. It was like old times. I haven't taken off the earrings you gave me. I have to tell you again, Lianne is so cute, and you're doing a great job! It was wonderful to see you with your family, your very own family. And Doron is terrific.

My brothers surprised me, in a good way. They've matured so much, and they're turning into responsible adults. I think our father's death forced them to take care of themselves and to take life seriously. My mother asked if she can visit us this summer. I think it would be amazing, it just depends on whether or not she can get the time off from work. I really hope she can.

Missing you,

Michal

φφφ

I couldn't stop thinking about our two weeks in Israel. A land where the sun is always shining, where I can look up into its brilliance and enjoy its warmth, a land where the sea is deep blue, where people speak my language. I knew that there were a lot of people who would look at me scornfully and tell me that if I stay in the United States for a few more years, I'll forget how to speak Hebrew like an Israeli, and anyway, what is there to miss? Israeli society is becoming more violent, people are lonelier and poorer than ever. And they're right, I know. But I don't want to sever myself from this country and be done with it. I don't want to, and I couldn't, because this country is part of who I am.

I realized that I need Israel more than it needs me. I need its warm-heartedness, its mutual involvement, its language. I need my family. I need the cultural bounty that only Israel can offer.

Everywhere I've been, in the entire world, I have never left a theater without feeling even more alienated. I walk out of the theater and my heart aches for Israeli's low-budget but high-quality productions that are ten times better than what I had just seen. I love the feeling of watching live theater that speaks to me in my language- not just the words, but the mentality. It makes me feel like I belong.

During my visit, I took my in-laws to see "Fiddler on the Roof." The musical tells the tragic story of the Jewish people, of the wandering Jew looking for a place to lay down roots. The protagonist, Tevye the Milkman, never loses his kindness, his optimism, and his pure soul, despite all the tragedies that strike his family. This story only heightened my desire to return to Israel, to my home, to accept it as it is, for better or for worse. The whole package. To recognize that, while every country in the world has both good qualities and bad, the place that I belong- the place that I love- is Israel.

May 18, 1992

Dearest Michalush,

Ever since you went back to Seattle, I've been trying, unsuccessfully, to understand. If you feel like Seattle isn't your home, why are you still there? I just don't see what it is that Israelis are looking for when they go abroad, especially after that terrible bombing at the Israeli consulate in Argentina. Yes, life here is complicated, to say the least, but this is your home, I am your home, your family is your home. Why aren't you here with me? Look, I understand, you're curious to see what it's like to live somewhere else, you want to see the world, but the bottom line is, you're just not happy. You miss Israel, your son is your mother's only grandchild, so why aren't you here?

Things here are fine, after a not-so-fine period. I had strep, and it took me two weeks to shake it off. I feel like I've returned to adolescence, with all its hormonal peaks and valleys. I'm going through all of it, except the acne, and it's bizarre. Doron's been walking on eggshells; he's afraid I'm going to eat him for lunch. It's getting better. Work is going wonderfully. I've managed to stay on schedule, and I'm starting to dabble in graphic design and public relations for an exhibit of women's drawings at a Tel Aviv gallery. I have learned that all of the stages in a woman's life can be inspiring: the fetal stage, infancy, childhood, adolescence, motherhood, and even old age. We women, I've concluded, are a very robust species.

I'm working with the women who are exhibiting their artwork, trying to learn as much as I can about them so I can present them in the best possible light, I'm really enjoying it. I was particularly impressed with an artist who moved here from Iraq not all that long ago; by the time she left, the Jewish community there had essentially disappeared. Her story is remarkable. Her father was the leader of the Jewish community in Baghdad. As you know, most of the Jews there moved to Israel in the mass Aliyah in 1950. Only a tiny group of Jews remained in Iraq- twenty, thirty at most- and in order to preserve their religion, older men had to marry young women, and vice versa, to keep them from converting to Islam.

She told me how, one by one, her friends disappeared. Almost all of them escaped, but her father was determined to be the last one out: he didn't want to leave a single Jew in Iraq without someone to defend them. One day, there was a murder in their neighborhood, and her father was arrested. When her mother heard what happened, she went to the courthouse to try to get him released. The artist was ten years old at the time; her older brother was twelve. While the two of them were home alone, the police decided to search the house. Fortunately, their good-hearted neighbors smuggled the children into their own houses and hid them under the beds. The woman remembers how she hadn't been able to keep her entire body hidden- part of it kept jutting out. The children stayed there all night until their mother returned. A few days later, their father was released.

After they finished high school, she and her brother- after promising to return to Iraq, and leaving their parents behind as collateral- were allowed to attend college in Holland, and from there they continued on to Israel. Her father died in Iraq, and not long ago, her mother managed to escape during the Gulf War and join her children in Israel. In her paintings, the artist expresses the fear she felt that night, and the sense of security she feels now that she lives in a democracy. It saddens me that freedom is not something we can take for granted, and I understand- now more than ever- how grateful we should be for our country.

OK, now that I'm finished with my Zionist diatribe, I'll get to the point: when are you coming back? I miss you so much, and I can't figure out how we ended up living so far away from each other. I simply can't grasp it.

Love,

Tamar

June 6, 1992

Seattle

Dear Tamari,

 All is well here. We're finally back in our routine, our internal clocks have reset themselves, and the only thing that throws us off is the cycle of seasons. Summer still hasn't arrived- I guess it never got the memo- and it's been raining pretty much non-stop for a month. Even the long-time Seattlites are complaining about how gray it is. Inside our little house, however, everything is fine. Believe it or not, I've even started taking Yonatan for walks in the rain. Now, whether or not it's raining, I take him out every afternoon. The sun sets very late; it's strange, having so many hours of daylight, especially after such a long, overcast winter. Even at ten at night, it's completely light outside (even if it's gray). It's a peculiar feeling. Yonatan refuses to go to bed. Every night, he gives me the same argument: "It's not night yet, I don't want to go to bed!" You try explaining to him that in the north, it can be nighttime and the sun can still be shining. These endless days make me crazy. I get very little sleep, which is both a good thing and a bad thing. On the one hand, I'm very productive, but on the other hand, the light makes it hard for me to fall asleep, even if I'm tired.

Yonatan loves pre-school, and he's already chattering away in English. Now that I have more time, I'm thinking that I might start working a little (assuming I can find a job without a work permit). I've also started going to the gym. My days are pretty full. I feel sick just thinking about all the political nonsense going on in Israel. It's nice to be so far from all that chaos. What do you think?

Will there ever be peace, or will we always live by the sword? The election is only two weeks away, and it's strange looking on from the side, not influencing the outcome, (not that I'm even certain which party I would support.)

How are all of you? How's work? Any chance you can come for a visit? I know it's both expensive and far, but we have room for you, and you won't have to spend any money on anything, so come!

June 23, 1992

Michal, Michal!!

I'm in heaven! It's three in the morning, and I'm wide awake. I'm so excited I can't even sleep. Rabin is our new prime minister! Finally, someone's talking about peace. I've had enough with all this war, and now that Rabin was elected, there's hope. We were all glued to our TV screens, and when the results were in, we celebrated with champagne. It's too bad you're not here; I know you would have been thrilled, too.

Other than that, everything is fine. Work is as stressful as ever, but it's interesting. Right now, I'm working on product design for a new company. It's challenging, and I'm working closely with both my clients and my boss. Sometimes I have to stay late, but Doron or his mother take care of Lianni, so it's fine. I miss her, and sometimes I'm completely drained by the time I come home, but she always revives me. I'm glad I went back to work. I think it was the right choice for me. A happy mother is better than a frustrated one.

I'm telling you, this child is hilarious. Yesterday she rolled over three times, and she was so impressed with herself. This morning, when I was trying to change her diaper, she rolled over again. I can no longer change her diaper on the changing table- it wouldn't be safe. Doron says she's a little devil, and he's right. I just hope she won't be quite as mischievous as me.

Thank you for the invitation, but I don't see how we can visit any time soon. The flight is so long, and I don't have the energy to do it with a baby. Besides, the tickets cost a fortune- who has that kind of money? I miss you, too. Maybe it's time for you to think about moving back? Come back, live near me, we can raise our kids together.

What are you doing now that Yonatan's in pre-school and everything is so quiet? What do you do all day?

So long for now, I love you, and I pray that peace will bring you back home,

Tamari

July 12, 1992

Seattle

Tamari,

After an endless winter, summer has finally arrived. I have some exciting news: I'm pregnant! I thought it would take some time, like it did with Yonatan, but we were successful right away. There don't seem to be any complications. I'm in my seventh week, and my jeans are starting to get tight around the belly, so I bought some maternity pants. Overall, I feel OK. I'm occasionally nauseated in the mornings, but it's always gone by noon.

Dan is working very hard, and I hardly ever see him. When it's nice outside, Yonatan and I go to the park, and when the weather's bad, we meet up with friends. He'll be in daycare for most of the summer, and I'm glad. They won't do an ultra-sound for another ten weeks: American doctors don't believe in doing procedures unless they're absolutely necessary. I'm debating whether or not to have an amniocentesis. The doctor recommends it, but I'm not sure it makes sense. I'm still young, and how likely is it that there will be something wrong with the baby? Plus the test itself is risky. What do you think?

We haven't told Yonatan yet. I don't want him to get his hopes up until we're sure that everything is as it should be. I also don't want him to have to wait for too long.

You asked me what I do all day. It's a good question. On the days when I'm teaching Hebrew to my private students, it's fine, but some days all I do is meet up with friends and run a few errands. It passes the time. My pace of life is definitely different from yours, for better or for worse. As of now, I still don't have a work permit. I'm thinking about going back to school to get some kind of degree, because even if I do get a permit, my license to work as a pediatric occupational therapist isn't valid here. I'd have to take all kinds of supplementary classes, and get a special permit. I'm not sure what to do, especially because we don't plan to be here for more than another two or three years. And yes, I can't wait to live near you. It will be awesome to spend our afternoons together. My mother's coming for a visit in a couple of weeks, and that should be wonderful. I hope she'll have a good time.

In terms of the elections: I'm not holding out much hope for real change. Everything looks so different from here. The constant fighting in the Middle East doesn't seem like it's going anywhere. Do you really think that at this point, someone's going to wisen up and make a change? Do you really believe the right will allow Rabin to make peace? I'm skeptical.

It's unbelievable how different life is in the United States. Here, everyone's biggest concern is the weather, followed by what they're planning to do over the weekend. I don't really get it. Everyone lives their own little life in their own little bubble. They don't obsess over politics; some of them don't have the slightest idea what's going on in the world. There are parts of the country that are so remote; I can't imagine what people do all day. Last week we went for a hike on Mount Rainier, which is essentially a giant, dormant volcano, and we passed some towns that were truly in the middle of nowhere. We stopped at a little diner, and while we were eating, all these teenagers barged in and start asking the owner all sorts of questions. Apparently, this was part of a game that the high school students played every year. Someone hides a straw doll, and the kids split up into groups and try to find it, with the help of a single clue. It's considered a real honor to find it first. Right before the senior prom, they burn the doll. That's about as exciting as things get around here.

America is so huge, and there are so many little towns tucked away; people live by themselves, and for themselves. When I compare it to our tiny, cramped little country, Israel reminds me of a little candy shop on the corner: it may not look like much, but it is precious, and it is up to us to protect it.

Kisses to everyone, I miss you so much.

Love,

Michal

φφφ

I lived in Washington for more than fourteen years, and all I ever
wanted was to go back to Israel. At first I waited patiently, but
little by little I started losing hope that we would ever return.
During our first years in the States, I believed Dan when he
promised me that eventually, we would go back. He always had a
good reason for putting it off: "There's no reserve duty here, and
it's safer, too. Can't you see that this crazy intifada is tearing the
country apart? Do you really want our children to grow up in a
place where they blow people up? Let's just wait until things calm
down a little." Also: "I just got a promotion at work. You're asking
me to give it up?" Or: "Maybe your mother should stay with us for
a few months." But the one that really sent me over the edge was
this: "Life has finally calmed down. Maybe it's time you found
something to keep you busy. After all, we have a good life here."
Who's this "we"? Doesn't it include me? And Dan would
elaborate: "You're always looking for something to grab onto, it's
not good for you to be by yourself. You're not in a good place."
And I heard what he was saying, and I convinced myself that he
was right. The problem was me. What was the matter with me?
Why wasn't I content? Life was wonderful and peaceful and calm.
I just had to look inside myself and find my own happiness. And
the anger boiled and bubbled inside of me.

I know that sometimes people say hurtful things unintentionally,
but the things Dan said percolated deep inside me, little by little,
until they paralyzed me. The problem was me. The problem was
that I was never satisfied. The problem was with me, not them.
Yonatan was content, Abigail was content, only I remained

unsatisfied. The problem was in me, it was something buried deep inside me, it had nothing to do with what was going on around me. The problem was in me. Did I say that already?

July 25, 1992

Seattle

My dear Tamari,

I have some sad news to tell you. In the thirteenth week of my pregnancy, I had a miscarriage. Everything had been going along fine, I'd even gone out and bought some maternity clothes, and then I went for an ultrasound and they couldn't find a heartbeat. It was awful. I can't stop crying, and Dan is at a complete loss. For two days, I walked around with a dead fetus inside me, two full days of misery. My baby died inside me, and I would have to eject it from my body. All I wanted was for it to be over so I could crawl back into my little hole, wrap myself in a blanket, and never leave. It's so hard to grasp. I am grieving over what could have been, what can no longer be. Why did this happen to me? Why? I mean, I did everything right: I slept, I rested, I tried to avoid stress... So why did it happen? My doctor says that most women who have children of their own had a miscarriage at some point. That's how common it is. And I didn't even know this kind of thing happened, I didn't know that those were the statistics- and now I am a statistic myself. I'm glad we never said anything to Yonatan; I have no idea how I would tell him that the baby was there and now it's gone.

It's true, I was able to get past my father's sudden death, but this time I feel completely defeated. Yonatan is spending a lot of time with Dan, who's taken some time off to be with us, but in a few days he has to go back to work. He suggested my mother come, but she can't take off from work right now. I feel so alone. Why aren't you here with me? I need you! Come right away!

Love,

Michal

August 3, 1992

My dearest Michali,

Your letter broke my heart. I called you the moment I got it. Why didn't you call me right away? I can't understand. I hope I was able to raise your spirits a bit over the phone yesterday, and I am so sorry that I can't be there with you. You are in my heart all the time. I feel helpless next to your pain. Of course it's a huge loss, but you have to focus on what you do have: Dan and Yonatan who fill your life with joy, and the good friends you've made in Seattle. It's hard to help you from here, and I hate it that you're so far away. What can I do to help? How can I make you feel better, other than visiting you, which, I'm deeply sorry to say, I can't do right now. Our financial situation isn't great, as you know; our mortgage is squeezing everything out of us, and we almost never go out. So as much as I would love to come, I just can't. Please don't be angry; if you were here, I would never leave your side.

What do the doctors say? Take time to heal. Try to fill your day with things that make you happy, and don't ever forget that you are loved.

I'm sure we'll talk again before you get this letter.

Much, much love,

Tamari

ϕϕϕ

A year before my Abby was born, I had a miscarriage. I have only dim memories of this whole episode, and quite honestly, I try not to think about it. The emotional pain was excruciating, and I felt utterly alone. The loss of a baby, even an unborn baby whom you've never even met, is devastating. When your body is able to carry a baby, to uplift and be uplifted, to hold and be held, it's a glorious feeling. But discovering that your body is also capable of such cruelty, both towards the baby and towards itself- that feeling is almost too hard to bear. My baby didn't make it past thirteen weeks, but for those thirteen weeks, I was in heaven. I loved the idea that Yonatan would have a brother or perhaps a sister. I loved the thought that our family was growing. I had always wanted a house filled with children's laughter. I wanted to feel like I was never alone, to feel complete. I felt such bliss knowing I was carrying a sweet little baby, created by the love of a man and a woman; when I was stripped of that bliss, it was truly unbearable.

The void inside and outside my body was palpable. When my body was emptied, all at once, not only did I lose the baby, but all the towers I had built in my mind came tumbling down: the baby's fragrance, its first laugh, the baby's room, the sounds of a mobile circling over its head, hugging the baby, holding it close, hearing it gurgle, a stronger marital bond, a friend for Yonatan... a huge loss that encompassed thousands of tiny losses.

Dan was as supportive as he could be, and my friends sent over food, picked up Yonatan from school, and tried to get me out of the house. But I locked myself in: I didn't want to see anyone, hear anyone, all I wanted was to bury my face in my pillow and curl up inside my down quilt. It was cold that summer; the sun rarely showed its face, the temperatures were low, and it rained constantly. I felt lost and sad and empty, and although I tried to pull myself together- and others tried as well- I remained inconsolable.

I missed my mother, and my dead father, and my brothers, and Hebrew, and I yearned to be back in Israel. I pounced on Dan, telling him I didn't want to live here anymore, and I wanted to go back to Israel, to go home. He didn't take me seriously; this was nothing more than an outburst of pent-up emotions, he said, a result of the hormones raging inside my body. Soon everything would calm down, and we could start thinking about trying again. Once I felt better, we could go on a trip, maybe even to Yellowstone Park, which was only a day's drive from here, a day and a half at most; maybe that would cheer me up. He also said that I should get out of the house more, rain was just rain, I wasn't going to melt. His words of encouragement didn't help. I just dug myself deeper into my hole and refused to be comforted.

Only two months later, we did go on a trip. It was the end of summer, right after my mother's visit, which I enjoyed but Dan found difficult. He felt like his personal space was being invaded, and that there wasn't any room in the house for him. We didn't go to Yellowstone, but to the beautiful, rocky Oregon coast. Every morning, the sea lions would sidle out of the water and sun themselves on the rocks. At low tide, we would take Yonatan to look at all the newly exposed sea creatures. The differences between low and high tide were striking. At low tide, not only could you see a whole slew of marine animals; you could also see people pushing metal detectors, searching for treasures under the sand. We strolled through quaint little towns, we slept in small inns, and when we came back, I discovered I was pregnant.

October 25, 1992

Seattle

Dear Tamari,

Thank you so much for all the support over these last difficult months, for your phone calls, for your time…. Without you, I could never have gotten through any of it, especially those first days, right after I lost the baby and I wanted to die. Some days were so bad they felt like they would never end, and it wasn't easy for me to emerge from the shock and sadness that had washed over me. If you hadn't called me almost daily, I don't know if I would have been able to function.

I'm writing with happy news, only this time I'm much more cautious and much less optimistic, though still hopeful. I'm pregnant. I just found out yesterday, and you're the first to find out (other than Dan, obviously).

I feel fine so far, but it's just the beginning- I haven't even seen the doctor yet. I figure I'm in my fourth or fifth week. It looks like the pregnancy began when we were on vacation in Oregon.

Our trip was fantastic. I'm glad we took the time to explore at our own pace. We relaxed when we wanted to, we took long walks along the beach, we rode dune buggies on the Newport shores, we toured a cheese factory (it's called "Tilamook"- it's pretty famous around here), we went out in low tide and looked at all the sea creatures, and we splashed around in high tide. In the mornings, we watched sea lions resting on giant rocks. Most of all, we enjoyed Yonatan's joy.

You won't believe who my mother ran into on the street last week: D'vir. I hear he looks terrific. He told my mother that- get this- he teaches at Haifa University. In the philosophy department! I almost fell out of my chair when she told me that. D'vir, a lecturer? With a doctorate in philosophy? His life is nothing like I imagined it would be. He's married, and he has a baby, only a few months old. He asked after me, and was shocked to hear that I was living abroad. Of course he sent regards, and even gave my mother his phone number and suggested I get in touch with him next time I visit, but I don't think I'll call him. What's the point?

How are things with you? I hope you're not working too hard. When can you visit already? Actually, it probably doesn't make sense for you to come right now. It's cold and rainy, and the winds are blowing like mad.

Love and miss you,

Michal

φφφ

As time went by, I had less and less contact with Israel, but in my
heart I remained as devoted as ever, especially after a visit. I
would come back from those visits with my spirit shattered. In
Israel, I saw the people I loved, soaked up the sun, hung out at the
beach, walked through the streets window-shopping and people-
watching. I took pleasure in the straightforwardness, the mutual
concern and involvement that I had missed so much. The warmth
of the Israeli people warmed my heart. When I returned to
Seattle, I felt like life had ground to a halt. And with each passing
year, the gap between what I felt on the inside and what I
experienced on the outside grew wider. In my heart, and in my
day-to-day life, I was "there"- in Israel. But my body knew full well
that it was stationed "here" in Seattle. I felt like a robot. I did
whatever was required: I tended to the house, the kids, and my
marriage, but there was always something hollow, something
dormant, in my heart. I asked myself, more than once, what I
should do. Should I continue to live like that, or should I take
action?

Aside from my mother and Dan's parents, nobody ever came to
visit; the flights were not only expensive, but long and difficult,
too. What young couple could afford to spend thousands of
dollars just to come visit? My brothers always talked about
coming, but it never happened, and the same was true of my
friends. Worst of all, it was true of Tamari, too. In the early years,
our friendship was as strong as ever- we made sure to write to
each other, to send each other photos of the kids, to talk on the
phone every now and then- but over time, we grew apart. I could

149

see how other people were filling up her life: she started talking about all the things she'd done with other people, the deep conversations they'd had, the trips they'd taken together... Her experiences were so different from mine. Even though we continued to see each other once a year and to write to each other, unintentionally and unknowingly, our worlds drifted apart. I know that she changed, and I assume I did as well. We marched to different rhythms, and grew in different directions. Tamari got promoted at work and was given even more responsibility, and she had three children. She was always busy. I thought of her as a career woman, a devoted mother, and a wonderful partner. Someone who craved new experiences, like taking jeep tours with her girlfriends. Whereas I... I had two kids, and I couldn't find myself, not in Seattle, not in my heart. The trips we took only intensified my longing to return to Israel. Yes, my kids kept me busy, but the feeling of emptiness only grew stronger with time. Who was I? Israelis considered me American, Americans considered me Israeli, and I felt like I didn't belong anywhere in the world.

Life went on. More accurately, life sailed by on a lovely, calm stream, surrounded by trees and grass and wildlife, so pastoral and at the same time so numbingly dull. After Abigail was born, I considered going back to school, but I kept thinking that we were there only temporarily, and that I might not be able to complete my studies. I looked for a short-term program that would be useful in both Seattle and Israel, but it never came to anything. The classes were huge and expensive, and I was afraid that if I went to school, it would damage the kids. After all, Dan was immersed in his world, which now included a number of charitable causes: feeding the hungry, protecting animals. (When he volunteered with the animals, the kids sometimes accompanied him.) He also helped organize parties and events for the Israelis living in Seattle. During the week, he was so busy with work that I hardly ever saw him, and the weekends were no less frenetic. I withdrew into my own world, amusing myself with all kinds of strategies for improving my life, but ultimately sticking to my safe, boring routine.

The whole time I lived in the States, I was troubled by the loss of my connection with Tamari. During the first few years, I called her frequently. She called me, too, from time to time, but gradually, our connection waned. Not all at once, not even sporadically, but slowly, painfully, painful to me in particular. I don't think she missed me all that much; she was so busy, after all. If she had missed me, she would have made more of an effort to stay in touch. The bond between me and my soul sister- between me and the best friend I ever had- softly drifted away, as if in a twilight sleep.

In the beginning, the fact that she never called didn't bother me. I fashioned all kinds of excuses for her: the cost of calling, the time difference. The notion that perhaps she should be calling, too, never even crossed my mind. I was in a better financial situation than she was, and so I never kept track. But like any interaction that isn't mutual, at some point, I don't remember when, I began to understand that my role in her life was getting smaller, whereas she remained my dearest and most beloved friend.

I decided not to call her for a week and see what happened: she didn't call. Then I began waiting even longer between calls. Our letters became less frequent.

At one point, Dan and I lent her and Doron a significant amount of money. In my naiveté, I imagined that this would bring us closer. In fact, it had the opposite result. Now she didn't see me as a friend, but as a collector, as someone to whom she owed a debt. Our e-mails- most of which were written by me- became less frequent. Finally I'd had enough. I stopped calling, I stopped writing, and when I finally moved back to Israel and locked myself in my little Tel Aviv apartment, I didn't even tell her I was there.

November 8, 1992

Tel Aviv

Hi Michali,

What's up? I hope everything is going well, and that your pregnancy is progressing smoothly. We're fine here, aside from the politics and the tragedies that are sweeping our country. I don't know how much you keep up with things, but a few days ago something awful happened at the military training camp in Tze'elim, during a staff exercise. Five soldiers were killed when a fellow soldier accidentally pulled the trigger. I think about what the families of those soldiers must be going through, and it scares me. How horrible and painful and incomprehensible it is, to send your child off to reserve duty for a couple of weeks and never get him back. I apologize for writing about something so sad, but the photos and interviews are all you see when you turn on the TV.

Lianni is a big girl already. She likes to pull herself up to standing and walk around the coffee table. Everyone says we're "moving up in life," meaning that now, anything she can touch has to be moved up to a higher shelf. Work is crazy as usual; I like my job, but sometimes the pressure is just too much.

Doron's doing OK, too, although I think he's fed up with his boss. He might start looking for a new job, which means our plans for a possible visit have to be put on indefinite hold. That's it for now, just wanted to send a quick note saying I love and miss you.

See you at some point...

Tamari

ϕϕϕ

As soon as Abigail was born, by caesarian section, I knew that I didn't want to live in Seattle anymore. I wanted to raise my children in Israel, in the place I grew up, near their uncles and my mother and Dan's parents, and most importantly, the only place where I felt like I belonged. When Dan came to visit me the day after the birth, dragging an emotional Yonatan behind him, I hissed between my teeth, "I want to go home. I'm sick of this." Dan thought I was referring to the hospital, but I made myself clear: "I want to go back to Israel. I don't want to raise our kids here." Dan laughed and said that of course we'd go back to Israel one day, he was sure of it; he must have thought that this vague reassurance would subdue the beast that had suddenly bared its claws. Then he took Abigail in his arms, stroked her face, and said, "Welcome to the world, my little American!" This only made me angrier.

On a cold, rainy day, I brought home a tiny package, with Abigail inside. The rage I felt towards Dan grew stronger by the day.

Abigail was a wonderful baby. I felt like she understood what I needed. She started sleeping through the night very early on, as if she were trying to compensate me for all the sleepless nights I'd endured when I was nursing Yonatan. She was a quiet baby, she ate well and slept well, at six weeks, she started smiling at everyone, a smile that progressed into a great rolling laugh. Her smile won over all our hearts, but nobody was more enchanted than Yonatan. Before I left the hospital, I called him over to my bedside and told him that from now on, he would never be alone.

He would always have a friend. Yonatan welcomed his sister-
Gayil, he called her- with joy. He wanted me to bring Gayil
wherever we went, and he was very proud of her. At playtime, he
would set some of his toys in front of her and include her in all his
games. When she started rolling over, he put his toys on the floor
in front of her, trying to tempt her to reach for them. And later
on, he would only go to a friend's house if Abigail could come,
too. I was so proud of my children, and I enjoyed them so much. I
could never have imagined that one day I would leave them
behind, that I would choose my homeland over them. As if I no
longer believed in love, in family, in friendship. My obligation was
to myself, and only to myself.

January 20, 1993

Dear Tamari,

It's a girl! I only found out today, at the ultrasound, and I'm just
thrilled. We have a daughter, a sweet, delicate daughter. Dan is
excited, too. We still haven't told Yonatan. I did tell him that I was
pregnant, but I told him it would be a long time before I knew if
he would have a brother or a sister. After the miscarriage, I don't
want to get his hopes up. Tamari, he is so big. He gets dressed by

himself and he plays nicely with others. He makes me proud and happy every single day. He's just a delightful child.

For now, I feel fine. Now that the morning sickness is over, I'm a bit more mobile, and if it weren't for the never-ending rain, I'm sure we'd go out more often.

The New Year began with torrents of rain, and a week ago there was so much snow that we couldn't even leave our houses. I have to admit, though, there was something very beautiful and peaceful about it. Dan bought a sled, and we met up with all the neighborhood kids at a great sledding hill. It was a blast! The holiday season is very colorful here. Everyone decorates their houses, the stores are packed, there are fir trees behind every window. It makes me realize how much I don't belong here. I know that there are plenty of people who would trade places with me in a minute, but I'm giving it two years, maximum, before we go back to our little country. I miss it so much! I don't know when our next visit will be; maybe this summer, after the baby is born. Now that I've accepted that you're not coming, the distance between us makes me even sadder. I'm lucky that I have some friends here who invite us over and who visit us; otherwise, I'd go crazy.

What's going on with you?

Kisses, Michal

2005

Spring has arrived. I love the smell of spring in Israel; it has a special fragrance unlike anywhere else in the world. Everything starts blooming again, in a tempest of colors and smells; the weather changes at a moment's notice. I put on my lightest, gauziest clothes, and step out into the world. The evenings are lovely, and I'm determined not to worry about whether or not Iris has returned, and not to wait for Roni to come home; instead, I will go out and stroll through the streets. In my heart, there is a nugget of contentedness; I release it into my tired body, tired from all the sadness, all the longing. I walk through the streets until I reach Yarkon Park. At this lovely time of day, children are still gliding back and forth on the swings, their mothers idly chatting. Fathers call their children over and hand them sandwiches, an improvised dinner for a spring evening.

My children are grown up, and they no longer frequent the park, but when they were little, I took them outside every chance I got. If the skies weren't bombarding the ground with their water, and the temperature was within the normal range, we would go out. I would pack up a bag of snacks, water, stale bread for the ducks, a ball, and sometimes bicycles. It was in the park that Yonatan and Abigail, in turn, learned to ride their bikes. It was the best part of the day: for me, a welcome reprieve, and for them, a chance to release some pent-up energy.

How I long for my children…. How I long for those years in which I could lift them up in my arms, hug them and kiss them. I long for the touch of my cheek on their smooth, beautiful cheeks, for their rolling laughter, for the feel of their tiny hands inside my hands.

157

Abigail was shy, and whenever we went somewhere new, she would nuzzle into my thigh.

Tears fill my eyes; I wipe them away immediately. I long for the scent of their bodies, the sound of their breathing at night. How peaceful they were, those years when my children were small, before they began to close their bedroom doors and cut themselves off from the rest of the world. When it came to anything sleep-related, Yonatan was the funnier of the two. He would complain that he wasn't the least bit tired, and he would try to look angry, but a smile would creep up along the edges of his mouth, and I knew that I could dissolve all his anger with a kind word, or with a game of "Who can brush teeth first?", or with tickling his belly. To this day, Yonatan is still ticklish. Our evening ritual was always the same: stopping whatever he was doing (never without a fight), showering, brushing his teeth, story-time, and lights out. More than once, he fell asleep before I even said good night. And if I had to step out of the room for a moment, to look for something or to answer the phone, I would almost always come back to find him sleeping the sleep of the just.

I sit on a green bench, inhale the smell of the flowers, close my eyes, and turn myself over to the voices of the children. Soon I will get up and go back to my little apartment, perhaps stopping at the café on the corner of my street.

"Michali, is that you?" I hear a familiar voice, and shake myself out of my reverie. Across from me stands Tamari. I haven't seen her in such a long time. I haven't heard from her, or about her. I stare at her for a minute, unsure what it is that I'm feeling. Maybe I'm just surprised to see her and I don't know how to react. I sit up straighter and look right at her.

"Yes, it's me," I answer. I'm not ready. I tug my purse closer to make room for her. She sits down, but not before apologizing for not having written in so long.

We sit there in silence. I wonder what I'll say to her if she asks me why I'm in Israel when it's not vacation, or why I didn't tell her I was there, even though I think her apology is sincere. We haven't been in touch for nine years. While I'm deliberating over what to say, she lets loose with a stream of words, barely stopping for breath. "I can't believe you're really here," she says. "I can't tell you how often I've thought about writing or calling, I'm so sorry we fell out of touch, I just can't believe it happened. And you look good, a little pale, maybe, but good, and there are so many things I want to tell you." She pauses for a moment and looks at me, making sure I'm listening. I am listening, but what does she want me to say? Where do I begin? Do I tell her how hurt I was that she borrowed such a large sum of money and "forgot" to pay it back? And by forgetting that, she also "forgot" me? She stopped answering my e-mails, didn't even return my calls. She just absented herself from my world, my closest friend, my sister, my love, my other half.

I feel like my heart is about to burst, and all the pain I had been holding in will course through my body until I overflow. I don't say anything. "Michali," she says, "say something."

I continue to sit there in silence. She takes both my hands in hers.

"Michali, please, say something." I pull my hands away.

"I'm sorry," I say, "I have to go." I pick up my purse and run. Tears are streaming down my face. I wipe my eyes with the edge of my

159

sleeve as I walk, and at some point I realize that I'm wailing like a cat in agony. I don't stop moving, not even for a minute; I walk fast, as if someone's chasing me. All I want to do is get back home, but home feels farther than ever, and the road stretches out before me without end. I speed up even more, and only when I can finally see my street, I stop to catch my breath. I wipe away my tears and bite down on my hand to keep myself from letting out a scream so loud it would shatter the night sky that has just appeared overhead. Once I've calmed down a bit, my steps grow slower and heavier, and when I finally reach my door, I fumble for my key, open the lock, barge inside, and slam the door behind me. I shuffle across the floor, all my strength completely depleted, and lie down on the cold stone, howling for my death.

February 15, 1993

Hi Tamari,

Lianni sounds so sweet over the phone. I can't believe she's already talking! I'm glad I was able to catch you on the phone, especially because you haven't responded to any of my letters, and I haven't heard from you in so long. Everyone here is fine. It hasn't stopped raining, but I'm doing my best to keep myself busy, and I'm enjoying my little family.

This week, I noticed that Yonatan has started speaking to me in English, mostly after I pick him up from pre-school. I have to remind him that at home, and with our family, we only speak Hebrew. I'm afraid he'll forget his Hebrew. Yonatan loves his school and his teacher, and so do I. I am very impressed by the school's educational philosophy: students are taught to respect each and every child, to give every child the space he or she needs, and say thank you, to feel grateful. Yonatan is also learning to write in English. On Fridays they have a special Shabbat program, and the children bake their own little Challot. I love having long weekends. Last weekend, Dan took Yonatan skiing nearby. They took a skiing lesson, and I stayed home. I can't tolerate the cold, and the sidewalks are so icy, I'm always afraid I'll slip and fall, even if I'm only going to our neighborhood café.

Dan and I are planning to surprise Yonatan with a trip to Disneyland. We're going in five weeks; I've already bought our airplane tickets. We'll wake him up in the morning, supposedly to take him to school, but instead, we'll take him to the airport. I reserved rooms in the Disney hotel, where he'll be surrounded by all of his beloved characters.

161

Dan works long hours every day, and by the time he gets home, he's exhausted. During the week, we hardly ever see him, but he tries to devote his weekends to us, and it's nice. It's also nice to be able to take vacations to all kinds of new places. Truthfully, what I like best about living here is being able to fill up your tank with gas and just drive and drive. It's such a huge country, and there is so much to see. I can't wait until we have time to explore even more.

Other than that- I wish I were closer. My mother told me that she can come for the birth, but can only stay for two weeks, because she has to get back to work. My brothers have no plans to visit, at least for now. I do hope they will come at some point.

If you have a chance, do you think you could buy a few Hebrew books and CD's to send over with my mother? I know it's still early, but I want to give you a head's up so you'll have time to plan.

Take care of yourself, and write. I hope you're not as overwhelmed as you were. Give my best to Doron.

Love you,

Michal

φφφ

The days passed slowly, with little upheaval. Long rainy days, and sleepless nights: the children were always getting sick. Days turned into months. I desperately wanted another child, but Dan wouldn't hear of it. I focused more and more on my children. I structured my whole life around their activities: carpools, classes, after-school programs, and friends. As their social lives intensified, my own friendships waned. I told myself I simply didn't have the time, but the truth was that as more Israelis moved to Seattle, the community started feeling like a kibbutz, and I didn't want to be a part of it.

The "new arrivals" that came every year chose to live in our neighborhood, which had a large contingent of Israelis. They sent their children to the same schools and signed them up for the same activities. The mothers hung out with each other, they celebrated the holidays together, and the more kibbutz-like the community became, the more I felt smothered. As the "kibbutz" expanded, I retreated into myself. Everyone knew everyone else, and instead of enticing me closer, it made me want to run away. I had experienced real kibbutz life, and I couldn't see myself as part of a kibbutz in Seattle.

Dan liked it, though, and he would often take the kids to different activities while I stayed home. Of all my many friends, with all their parties and events, only one friendship survived. To this day, Noga is one of my dearest friends, and she is the only one from that enormous community- the community I belonged to- who remains a part of my life.

Ironically, I felt a stronger connection to the American mothers at the school. These women gave me space to breathe, and our friendships were undemanding and comfortable. I could go two years without speaking to someone, and nobody would hold it against me. To the contrary, they offered support and understanding, and they never judged me, something I deeply appreciated. But these friendships, while uncomplicated, were not particularly close. The American women respected my privacy, and I theirs, and as a result I couldn't talk to them about my personal problems, my feelings of disquietude, my pain and frustration. Instead, we limited our conversation to movies, plays, harmless gossip- anything that wasn't personal.

I avoided my Israeli friends more than ever. In addition to my distaste for the communal life, I was afraid of what other people might be saying about my highly imperfect family. What if they uncovered the truth? What if they realized that my marriage was a farce, that the emperor had no clothes, and that we had nothing to offer? They would want nothing to do with us.

And so I abandoned them before they could abandon me. That was the only way I could maintain my dignity, and keep my family together. I was afraid to expose myself to the scrutiny of these people, afraid of what they might pressure me to do. In the end, people form close friendships with those who are similar to them, and I wasn't like any of the people surrounding me.

Meanwhile, Dan, who was warm and generous with the outside world, drifted further and further away from us. He was less present in our lives; he was always finding new things to keep him busy. He became a biking fanatic, and on weekends he would go riding with other bikers. We rarely saw him. I could feel that our paths were diverging. In the beginning I did everything I could to narrow the gap between us, but Dan, who didn't think that anything had changed, insisted that he still loved me as much as he did when we first met. Those kinds of assurances only intensified my feelings of alienation. Just as I rejected the superficiality of the American lifestyle, I remained untouched by his empty words. I didn't believe in him; I didn't believe him.

Love isn't measured in words, but in deeds, and his actions didn't live up to his words. If he loved me, why did he pull away from me? If he loved me, why did he spend all his free time away from me and our children? If he loved me, why didn't he notice my unhappiness? I withdrew into myself, into my bitterness. My relationship was deteriorating. The years were going by, and we were still in Seattle, so far away, both geographically and emotionally. Nothing made me feel at home, not even the house I lived in. Even my own four walls had turned against me.

March 12, 1993

Seattle

Hey Tamari,

How's it going? Everything here is relatively fine, considering how much worse it could be. I haven't heard from you in a long time, and whenever I call you, you're not home. Maybe you never realized that I called: I didn't leave a message, because I didn't want to worry you. Anyway, it all started six weeks ago, when I felt some slight pain. (We were supposed to fly to California two days later, but we ended up cancelling the trip. I hope we'll have another chance to take Yonatan to Disneyworld, maybe after the baby is born.)

Briefly, here's what happened: my blood pressure spiked, and I was put on bed rest. I'm resting as much as I can, and I'm trying not to carry anything and not to pick up Yonatan (who doesn't really understand why I'm lying in bed instead of taking him to the park). My friends are doing their best to help me- sometimes they take Yonatan for the afternoon. The truth is, I prefer it when he's home with me. He's at pre-school most of the day, and I miss him. I'm pretty lonely, and I enjoy his company. Dan continues to come home at an ungodly hour, and I hardly ever see him. True, he calls to check on me a few times a day, and sometimes we have lunch together, but it's not enough, He's busy on the weekends, too. I'm trying to convince him to cut back on his commitments a little, at least for now, but it doesn't seem to be working.

I ache with loneliness, and I want to go home to Mother. Can you believe I feel this way? I never expected to miss her this much. All

I want is for her to pamper me a little, to mother me, to cook me a hot meal, or just to have a conversation with me.

I spend most of my time watching TV; I know everything there is to know about morning talk shows. Once in a while I'll borrow a movie from the library, and I read a ton. Still, between the constant discomfort and the endless exhaustion, the eight remaining weeks of bed rest feel like they'll never end. Every day feels like a year, and I am sad and alone. It's hard not to think about the fact that I could be going through this pregnancy with you and my mother and my brothers nearby, in a land where there is infinite sunshine and the bluest sea.

Maybe you'll reconsider and come for a visit anyway?

I love you and miss you,

Michal

April 22, 1993

Tel Aviv

Dear Michal,

I hope you're hanging in there. I know it's not easy, lying there in bed when the rest of the world is carrying on without you. I'm so sorry I can't be there. The truth is, even if I could get a few days off from work, I probably couldn't come anyway. It's so far away. A day there, a day back, a ten-hour time difference... not to mention the cost of the tickets. Michali, I can't even remember the last time Doron and I took a vacation. Life here is so frantic, and the salaries are ridiculous. We barely make it to the end of the month, and even that is only with the assistance of Doron's parents, who are helping us pay off our enormous mortgage. I am so sorry. If things were different, I would definitely come, but I'm sure you understand that right now, it's just not possible.

I'm glad I was finally able to talk to you, and as you can see, I'm writing back. It's quite late: one in the morning. I finished my chores for the day, and in another five hours I have to get up for work. The house is still, and everyone's asleep. This is my favorite time of day. True, it means I have to drag myself out of bed in the morning, but it's a small price to pay for these quiet hours, when everyone else has fallen asleep. I can get a lot done. Doron and I divide up the household chores, but I always do my share at night. Like folding the endless mountains of laundry, for example, those are sitting there waiting, just for me. It gives me a chance to think.

Lianni has become such a big girl. She'll be starting pre-school soon, before the summer, (when Doron's parents are taking a long trip to Canada). I think it will be good for her. She needs to be with other kids, even if the love that she gets from her teacher will be nothing compared to the love that is heaped upon her by Grandma Ruti.

Doron and I are talking about having another child. We don't want a big age gap between the kids, but we're still on the fence: we're not sure we can swing it financially. Doron says that this isn't a good enough reason and we'll find a way to make it work, just like everyone else does.

Darling Michali, I worry about you. You have to remember that this is just temporary. Yes, it's hard to spend your day just lying there, not doing anything, but it has its benefits, too. Eight weeks from now, after the baby is born, you'll wish you had time to read books and watch movies. The main thing, Michali, is to focus on what matters and to enjoy what you have, and what you have is an amazing family to bring you comfort and pride.

Love you,

Tamari

Oh, I almost forgot. Guess who sends his regards? D'vir! I bumped into him yesterday at a café near my office. He was very interested in how you're doing- he asked a lot of questions, and wants you to get in touch with him next time you're here. He still lives in Haifa, and he's teaching Philosophy of the Far-East at the university. He has a daughter named Noga. Sweet name, don't you think?

That's it for today. Now I really have to hit the sack.

Love, Tamari

May 5, 1993

Seattle

Dear Tamari,

I'm getting towards the end of my pregnancy, and I'm still spending most of it lying flat on my back. However, I can finally see the light at the end of the tunnel, only six more weeks. It's just that each day feels like a year. I'm trying to think about all the good things in my life, and the truth is I have a lot to appreciate, and a lot to be proud of. Yonatan is amazing and smart and good; he's bursting with love and affection. Wherever I lie down, there he is. If I'm in the room, he'll bring his toys to me, and if I drift off, I wake up to find him next to me, playing quietly so as not to wake me up. How can a four and a half year old boy be so sensitive? Every time I see him acting this way, I tear up. Yonatan fills my world with joy, and I am grateful to Dan every day for giving me this gift.

These past few days, Dan's been making an effort to get home earlier. Yonatan and I both need him more and it's nice to have him around. He also tries to take on the shopping and the cooking when I'm not feeling well. I'm really enjoying my family, Tamari. Thank you so much for opening my eyes. Now do you understand why I miss you so much? Your vitality, and your ability to put things in perspective, is a special gift that only you have.

My mother calls me every day. She worries about me, too. I asked her to come for longer this time, and fortunately she was able to extend her vacation to three weeks. I already ordered her ticket, and I'm counting the days until she gets here. My doctor is considering inducing me at the end of the thirty-seventh week. By then the baby will be big enough, he says, and her lungs will be fully developed. All we can do now is pray for me to get through this. It's not easy, physically or emotionally.

My doctor is both capable and compassionate. In Israel, when I was pregnant with Yonatan, the doctor saw me as nothing more than an incubator. And because my pregnancies are so complicated, my psyche needs to be cared for as well as my body. This much I will say for the Israeli doctor: he delivered Yonatan with no complications, and he gave me the name of the doctor here, whom I call my angel. I'm in week 32, and we're starting to think about names. Any ideas? We're thinking about Maya, Noa, Avishag, and Abigail. Noa's not really an option, because here it sounds like a boy's name (think Noah from the Bible). Maya sounds sweet, but Mayas are a dime a dozen here. Avishag- the Shunamite who kept King David warm in his old age- appeals to me, as does Abigail (David's wife). I love Biblical names, and I just realized that Yonatan, Avishag and Abigail are all connected to King David.

The days are long, but spring refuses to arrive. Lots of rainy days, not much sunshine... it's not easy for us Israelis, but Yonatan doesn't even blink an eye.

Thanks for the update on D'vir. I do think about him from time to time, but I'm not sure I want to see him. It's been ten years since I last saw him, and people change. Maybe I'd be disappointed, and that would be awful. But what if I fell in love with him again? That would be even worse.

I miss you so much. I'm really hoping to come for the holidays with the kids (yes, kids, plural! I can't believe it...).

Love you, and hope to see you soon,

Michal

2005

Inside my apartment, the phone rings. Usually it's a wrong number or a sales call. My brothers don't call me anymore. They've finally accepted that I don't want to have anything to do with them, and after a long talk, we agreed that if I ever changed my mind, I would get in touch with them. I don't celebrate any of the holidays, and Shabbat is just like any other day, just a little quieter. I want all my days to feel the same. Mostly, what I want is for this pain that's burning inside me to go away.

Shabbat and holidays are the worst. The peacefulness all around me…. Through the open windows, I hear the sound of children playing and singing, and it reminds me of my own abandonment, of the deep and relentless void within me. Those days are almost too much to bear. I spend most of the day in bed, trying to sleep away as much of it as possible. I try to dream about my far-off and beloved children. Day turns into night, and night into day. Sometimes my neighbors invite me for a holiday meal, but I always decline. I don't want anyone else to find out about my disgrace and my pain.

Were it not for my neighbors, I would surely go mad. Their routines are what fill up my life. Roni's back from reserve duty, and he seems a little less preoccupied. He's still in a hurry most of the time, rushing in and out of his house, but sometimes he'll stand in the hallway or the front yard and chat with me. I don't tell him anything about me, and I don't give him a chance to ask. I fill up the conversation by asking him questions and telling him how much Na'ama has grown and how endearing she is. I had always thought of him as an accountant, but I was relieved to find out that he doesn't work with numbers, but with people.

When the phone rang, I was in the kitchen, and I took my time answering it. It stopped ringing, then started again. This time I picked up.

"Michali, it's me. Please don't hang up."

"How did you find me? What do you want?" My response to this familiar voice was chilly and terse.

"Dan gave me your number. Please, Michali, just give me two minutes." Her tone was authoritative; she didn't let me get a word in edgewise. I think if she hadn't sounded so sure of herself, I would have hung up on her.

I responded so quickly, even I was taken aback. "You have two minutes."

"I know I was wrong, and I'm asking for your forgiveness," she said bluntly. "I'm sorry we lost touch, I have no excuse, and I love you."

My eyes filled with tears. If she'd started fishing around for excuses, I wouldn't have stayed on the line, but when she asked me, in such a straightforward way, to forgive her, a chunk of my bitterness melted away. I tried to stifle my sobs: I didn't want her to know I was crying.

"Do you forgive me?" I couldn't answer; I was choking on my tears.

"Michali?" she continued. "You're still there, right?"

"Yes," I sputtered, "I'm still here." When I think back on it now, what I was really trying to say is that I had always been there: for her, for Dan, for the kids, for my mother, for my brothers, for everyone and their uncle. But what about for me? Who the hell had been there for me?

"Call me tomorrow," I said, and before I could change my mind, I hung up. Not because I was trying to punish her for her betrayal, but because I didn't want this to be easy for her. I wanted her to make an effort; I needed to know that I was worth the effort.

June 27, 1993

Hi Tamari,

We're home! Abigail and I are finally home. Thank you for the flowers and the beautiful note; they made me very happy. Like I told you on the phone, it was a difficult labor, but it was worth every minute. Abigail is amazing. I'd forgotten how it feels to hold such a tiny person in your arms. She is so small and so sweet. I'm enclosing some photos that Dan took at the hospital. See the worried expression on Yonatan's face when he looks at Abigail. Isn't it funny? I think he's already looking out for her like a good big brother. He was so excited when Dan brought him to the hospital to see us. He touched her so lightly, like he could tell how small and fragile she was. My mother's already gone back to Israel. It was so wonderful to have her here, and I miss her- and you- so much.

Life has pretty much returned to normal. I try to divide my attention between the two kids, but the truth is, if Yonatan needs me, I'll go to him first, even if Abigail is crying. I love watching him try to play with her, as if they're the same age. He talks to her, he strokes her face. When he watches TV, he asks me to put her down next to him so they can watch together.

I talked to Dan about visiting Israel, but he says he can't take any more vacation, and I'm scared to fly alone with both kids. If I can't work it out any other way, maybe I'll just grit my teeth and take the kids by myself. I don't see Dan and me visiting together.

I miss so many things about Israel: the language, the people, the music, the rhythm of life. Everything here is so laid back, I feel like

I'm sleeping even when I'm awake. Maybe it's because I don't sleep well, but I think it's because everything here is so sleepy....

What's going on with you? How are Doron and the little one? Did you sign her up for pre-school? What are your plans, anyway? Maybe a visit to our neck of the woods?

Until then, take care.

Love you and miss you, Michal

October 15, 1993

Hey Tamari,

We came home to rain and cold and the ever-present grayness. The fall colors are beautiful and wistful, as wistful as me. I can't enjoy the leaves, not even for a minute. All I want to do is grab my kids and get on the next plane back to Israel. I'm so proud of myself for being brave enough to fly alone with the kids. The flight home was as easy as the flight there. Yonatan is already accustomed to long flights. I pack lots of books and toys and workbooks and (of course) snacks, and he has his own private TV screen. On the flight home, he slept and played and kept himself occupied, this little sweetheart of mine. Abigail slept most of the way, and now she's all mixed up, sleeping during the day, wide awake at night…. It will work itself out.

I can't tell you how amazing it was being in Israel. I loved celebrating the holidays, seeing my extended family, and of course spending time with you. Lianni's terrific, and you and Doron are fantastic parents. No wonder Lianne is so full of life! Her rolling laughter is enchanting- did you see how Yonatan fell in love with her? The sun and the sea warmed my heart, and the trip to Jerusalem was unforgettable. Thank you for that wonderful day. I loved the shuk, the smells, the sounds, the Old City. I loved visiting the Western Wall. I hope that the note I stuck in the cracks between the stones will go up to heaven, then come back down to earth and across the sea and convince Dan to bring us back home.

For now, Dan is consumed by his work. His life has become so tranquil- no reserve duty, no terrorist attacks- and he loves it. He doesn't even want to hear about returning to Israel. He says we have to wait and see what happens with this Intifada, and with Lebanon, and we can't go back until things calm down.

My Seattle friends try to distract me by taking me on all these fun outings. Tomorrow, my friend and I are taking the kids to the Science Center. Once again, it's school vacation. Personally, I like having Yonatan at home, but some of the mothers complain that there are too many days off. Maybe this trip to the museum will cheer me up. And maybe it will help our marriage, too. Dan is furious that I came back feeling so bitter. He had hoped the trip would make me happier, but it turns out that when I returned- after leaving him alone for three weeks- I was even gloomier than I'd been before.

What he refuses to understand is that the solution is simple: I want to go home. As soon as I'm back in Israel, the smile will be back on my face. I tell him this, but it falls on deaf ears.

OK, that's all for now.

Write soon.

Love, Me

φφφ

I had waited for almost fifteen years, and I didn't want to wait anymore. As time passed, my dream of returning to Israel felt more and more remote. My children were Americans; visiting Israel once a year didn't make them Israeli. The older they got, the more connected they felt to their native land- which wasn't Israel. I never wanted it to turn out this way. Each year, I became lonelier, more resentful; I had no inner peace. While Dan continued to live his full and colorful life, I drifted away from him, and he from me, although he insisted that he still loved me. I wondered if he was telling the truth. It didn't feel like he was giving me enough love, or enough of his precious time.

He was so busy with all his activities that he had no room for us. He volunteered to chair local fundraisers and to feed the hungry. He loved cycling, and was practically addicted to bike trips with his friends. He was promoted at work. He hardly spent any time with us. When I complained about this, he pounced on me. If I had something to keep me busy, he said, I wouldn't have to whine all the time.

My life with Dan was a disappointment, but I continued to cling to my kids. Ultimately, they, too, rebelled. They were embarrassed by my Israeli accent and asked me not to speak Hebrew in front of their friends. It reminded me of my own childhood, how ashamed I was of my parents' Iraqi and Romanian accents, how embarrassing it was when they spoke in any language other than Hebrew.

And it wasn't just my accent. My children began fighting with me about everything. At first I dismissed it as a normal stage of adolescence, but little by little, I found myself feeling like a stranger in my own home.

2005

The day after my conversation with Tamari, I got an early start. I packed a book and a blanket, and set out to spend the day lazing in the grass in Yarkon Park. Afterwards, I thought, I might do some shopping. I would have done anything, as long as I didn't have to stay home waiting for Tamari to call. The walls of my house were closing in on me like a prison, and I wanted to get out. It was spring, and the weather was cool and comfortable. It was nice to walk down the old side streets of Tel Aviv. I stopped at a kiosk and bought a glass of fresh-squeezed carrot juice. I sat on a bench on the sidewalk and listened to the sounds that surrounded me: people coming and going, children shouting, birds chirping, cars and trucks rumbling by. I liked to watch the people, the younger ones always in a rush, mothers with strollers walking along purposefully, old people inching their way in front of me. Every stage of life, I thought, is beautiful in its own way. Life is beautiful. But what about my life? I tried not to think about my children, but the harder I tried, the more they invaded my memories and my emotions, and I barely managed to stop myself from crying.

I longed to hear their voices, to see their faces when they laughed, or when they cried, or when they were angry. I thought about all the pain I caused them, even though I'd had no choice. My children and my husband wouldn't even contemplate returning to Israel. Every time I mentioned it, all three of them attacked me, as if my idea was absolutely ludicrous. Of course, the current situation is equally preposterous: a mother of two children living on the other side of the world, unable to see her or hear her voice.

Dan is unmoved by the memory of our first years together, when I followed him through the desert to a life of loneliness and alienation. He refuses to forgive me for abandoning him. Many months have passed since I saw my children, and he won't let me talk to them. He made one thing very clear: if I ever want to see my kids again, it has to be on their territory. He is so intent on punishing me that he refuses to visit Israel; he doesn't understand that he is punishing the children, too, as well as his own parents, who miss their grandchildren terribly. Sometimes I wonder what happened to the love that he used to feel for me. There is no more mercy in his heart. Whatever mercy he had he channeled towards the outside world, and nothing was left for us, his little family, for me, especially. Like a beggar at the gate, I hoarded his few remaining shreds of kindness; like a beggar at the gate, I collected the small remnants of his precious time. What happened to the wellsprings of love and generosity that used to sustain our home? Everything he had to give, he gave to strangers; there was nothing left for us. Charity begins at home, I told him, but this sentiment only pushed him further away. Eventually, I stopped making demands of him; I immersed myself in my own affairs and stayed away from his hurtful presence.

I've changed over the last few months. I'm not the same dependent woman who relies on her husband's kindness. I live independently; I've even opened my own bank account. I acquired my own checkbook and my own credit card, and I did so all by myself. I pay my bills on time, despite the fact that my account is constantly shrinking. I had always assumed that I couldn't manage all the various responsibilities without someone else's help, but I found that I possess a strength I never knew I had. When I run out of money, I'll have to get a job. Maybe I'll work in my field, even though it's been more than sixteen years. Or maybe I can offer support to other women who've been emotionally neglected by their husbands. But until I've recovered from the dual abandonment- my abandonment of my family, and my family's abandonment of me- I don't have any strength to spare for other people.

I continue strolling through the streets, stopping to gaze into shop windows, giving some spare change to a homeless man. I decide not to go to the park as I'd been planning to do, but to the beach instead. I haven't been to the beach in quite some time, and the smell of the sea air calls to me. Without realizing it, I quicken my step, eager to get to the beach as soon as possible, and when I get there, I spread out my blanket and flop down upon it. I open my arms, then wrap them around my body, embracing myself. I hear laughter escaping through my lips; I don't know where it came from, and I don't care. I'm at the beach on a warm spring day in the land that I love. I refuse to let the sad thoughts surface. For a few minutes, I am content.

January 1, 1994

Seattle

A New (secular) Year. The streets are decorated, and Christmas music can still be heard all through the city. This is the season I dislike the most. The holidays are very family-oriented. The bustling airports, the jam-packed stores, the cloying music: all of it makes me dizzy. It's very cold, and it's been weeks since we've seen the sun. I try to go outside as little as possible, and I miss my home and my family....

I take comfort in my sweet children. A few days ago, Yonatan told me that when he grows up, he wants to be a Christian. When I asked him why, he said that Christian children get lots of presents. It made me laugh, but it hurt me, too. Would he even have thought of such a thing if he were living in Israel? I imagine that most Israeli boys his age assume that everyone in the world is Jewish, and that it would be a big deal to even meet a non-Jewish person. On the one hand, Americans believe in the separation of church and state, but at the same time, the Christian holidays are everywhere. In school, walking down the street... it's simply impossible to ignore them.

The Jews here have come up with a solution that I find outrageous. They give their children presents every night of Chanukah. Eight nights of presents- take that, Christians! In my opinion, it only makes things worse. The children end up focusing on the material aspects of the holiday rather than on other, more important values. And people who can't afford to give their kids gifts every night for eight nights feel their poverty more acutely than ever.

During the holiday season, I go out of my way to teach Yonatan about the Jewish holidays and their significance. I try to make them concrete, so he can relate to them. This Chanukah, we decorated the house together, lit candles, invited the neighbors for latkes and jelly donuts. I wanted to show him that our holidays are just as much fun as the Christian ones. Not only did I tell him the story of Chanukah, I also bought him a warrior's costume, and when he wore it, I called him "my little Maccabee." I think Yonatan is confused: I'm telling him one thing, but all around him, he's seeing something different. I hope we'll be able to celebrate next Chanukah in Israel.

Abigail is already six months old. I put toys down in front of her, and she crawls over to get them. Then she rolls onto her back and chews the toys like a happy little puppy. Her beautiful blue eyes remind me of my father. I'm glad that there's a part of him that has made its way into my everyday life.

Between work and volunteering, Dan is as busy as ever. We're planning a trip to Hawaii next month, and I hope that this time we don't end up cancelling.

What's new with you? It was great talking to you on the phone last week- I just wish we could do it more often.

Hoping to hear from you soon,

Love,

Michal

February 12, 1994

Tel Aviv

Hi Michali,

I've been meaning to write for a while. I hope all is well. Life here is very hectic- I feel like I can't get anything done. During the week, I never get home before six, and by then I'm exhausted. Doron comes home even later. We give Lianni a quick dinner and shower, then I collapse into bed until the following day. We spend most of our weekends with our parents, so we have no time for our own relationship or for the outside world.

You wrote about the Christian holidays. Let me tell you, I would give anything to be in the States during the holiday season. I love the decorations, the ceremonies... I don't really understand what you're complaining about. All it means is that you have more holidays to celebrate, more days off, more festivities to add some color to our grey lives. Unfortunately, I don't see us coming this year: our mortgage is squeezing our wallets and our souls.

Lianni's gotten big, and she has quite a vocabulary. She is overflowing with love, and she brings us so much joy. Even though she loves going to pre-school, she cries when I leave. She has an easier time when Doron takes her, so I usually ask him to bring her to school, which means I lose even more precious time with her. I like my job, but I never imagined how guilty it would make me feel. That's what I envy most about your life. You can be with your kids whenever you want; wherever they go, you can accompany them. The teacher's always telling me about all the developmental milestones I'm missing. But I love my work, and we need the money. We really couldn't get by without my salary. I suppose everything has its pros and cons....

When are you coming? I hope it's soon.

Hugs and kisses to everyone,

Tamar

P.S. I saw D'vir again. He asked after you, as always. He wants you to get in touch with him next time you're here. It seems to me that even now, after all these years, if you gave him the slightest hint of interest, he'd drop everything and come running.

φφφ

As the years went by, I became increasingly frustrated, and as my frustration grew, so did my bitterness. I turned inward, closing myself off from the outside world. To others, I must have looked like a dedicated mother and a loyal wife: PTA meetings, after-school activities, cleaning the house, shopping, cooking... that was the stuff of my daily life. I never complained about the tedium that was gradually overtaking me. Deep down, I kept dreaming about the day I would get on a plane and fly away from here, to my country. I brought up the subject every year, but it was never the right time. My role, it seemed, was to understand, to sit patiently, and to find something to keep me busy. (Something, of course, that didn't interfere with the lives of my husband and children.)

Then one day, I found myself thinking about death. My kids were being fresh and contemptuous, my husband wasn't home, as usual, and all I could do was sit and wait. I felt like the storybook character "The Scatterbrain from Kfar Azar," who boards an unmoving train and waits for something to happen. I couldn't go on like this.

I wanted to die; I even had a plan for how I would kill myself. The more I thought about death, the more terrified I became. One night, I didn't sleep a wink; I just roamed through my house like a sleepwalker. Dan was sleeping like a baby, and he didn't even notice that I wasn't lying there next to him. Or perhaps he was just pretending to be asleep so he wouldn't have to argue with me. I don't know what he was doing, or why, and I'm not even going to try to understand his behavior. All I know is that even though I was in my own house, surrounded by my own family, it was one of the loneliest nights of my life.

When the sun finally rose, I was utterly exhausted. I asked Dan if he could take the kids to school, but he refused, saying he had a long day ahead of him, and unlike me, he didn't have the luxury of coming back home and taking a nap.

That morning, Yonatan and Abigail argued about every possible thing, and they treated me the same way they'd been treating me for years: like a glorified servant. And that morning, I knew it had to end. One way or another, I had to escape. I could think of two possible exit strategies: I could leave the world or I could leave my house. Thankfully, I managed to choose the second option, and after I dropped off the kids, I went home and packed up a small suitcase with some clothes, some money, and my passport. Then I sat down to write a letter to Dan and the children. I told them I was going to Israel, and they shouldn't try to find me. I would contact them when I was ready. I left the letter on the dining room table, took one last look at the house that had been my sanctuary- or perhaps my prison- for so many years, and, feeling lighter than ever, walked out the door.

April, 1994
Passover (the holiday of freedom)

Seattle

Dear Tamari,

You have no idea how much I miss Israel, and my family, and you. It's Passover, and once again I feel isolated and resentful. I've lost so much: my kids, who are becoming so American; my brothers; my mother. The holidays are particularly hard, knowing that my entire family is in Israel, sitting around the table, reading the story of the Exodus. I don't know why we're still here. When will it be time for our own exodus?

We had the Seder with our friends Noa and Ron, a lovely couple, whose kids are the same age as Yonatan and Abigail. Our children play together after school, and go to the same Gymboree classes. Getting out of the house and meeting up with other families is good for the kids, and for me, too.

Glad to hear things are going well. As of now, I have no idea when we're going to visit. The flight is long and expensive, and flying with two kids is very challenging, with the long sleepless nights in both directions. Dan's not planning on coming with us, so it looks like we're going to have to wait for a better time.

How are all of you? How was your Seder? Your holiday?

If you see D'vir again, give him my regards. What's he up to these days?

Lots of love,

Me!

October 20, 1994

Dear Michal,

We haven't been in touch for a while. Life is hectic, and I get so little done. I have more work than ever, and very little free time. Being pregnant (I'm already in week 33) doesn't help. I think we have to consider moving to a bigger apartment, but Doron insists that we don't have enough money. It's going to be cramped; I hope it's manageable with two kids. I'm under so much stress, sometimes it keeps me up all night. Our mortgage is killing us, as you know; it's hard enough with one kid to support, much less two.

This pregnancy came as a complete surprise. I'm really not ready for another kid- I can barely manage with Lianne. It makes Doron crazy. "How can you not want more kids?" He doesn't understand. Sometimes I even think he's angry. I just don't see things the way he does. Saying something's going to be OK doesn't mean it's actually going to be OK.

I feel like there's something wrong with me. Everyone's congratulating me, everyone's all excited, they can't wait for the birth… and I don't even want to hear a word about it. I keep trying to push it off in my mind. As long as I don't know the sex, I can tell myself that it's not a real person yet, just something painful and annoying that gives you heartburn. Part of me wants this creature out of my body already, but another part of me wants it to stay inside me forever so it can't mess up my life.

How am I going to cope with two kids and a job? Doron's hardly working these days, and whatever money we do have, he wastes on all kinds of nonsense. He is so irresponsible.

I've been missing you so much lately. I know you could calm me down and cheer me up, and then after the birth we could get together and really talk. Maybe you'd help me out once in a while, like you did last time you were here. You took charge for an entire night, and I was finally able to get some sleep; when I got up the next morning I felt like a new person. You're so far away, and I'm so desperate. When are you coming?

Love, Tamari

2005

She came. Later that afternoon, after I had returned from the beach and taken a short nap, I heard a faint knock on the door. I thought it might be her, but I couldn't be sure. I mean, it's not like my neighbors come knocking- they have nothing to do with me. Maybe someone was lost and needed my help? I deliberated over whether or not to let the outside world burst into the sealed fortress that I had constructed for myself. I looked through the peephole, and there she was, standing, waiting. I backed away from the door, trying to decide if I should open it at all; maybe I'd just let her stand there until she finally gave up and left. But I summoned my courage and walked to the door. It was only a few feet from the living room, but it felt like a mile. I didn't know what I would say to her (or if I would say anything at all). After all, just yesterday I had run away from her. I didn't know if I'd be able to meet her gaze. What I feared above all was that I would fall apart in front of her, and I really didn't want that to happen.

She was standing there, in jeans and a turquoise cotton t-shirt that brought out the color of her eyes. A thought raced through my head: she's as pretty as ever. She was pressed against the wall, as if she was trying to brace herself against my anger, but I didn't get angry; I didn't say a word. I just looked at her. I noticed that the laugh lines on her face had been replaced by new, deeper wrinkles. Were they wrinkles of bitterness? Of hardship? How she has aged over the years, I thought in those few fleeting seconds, my hand still on the doorknob like I was about to slam the door on an intruder.

"Michali," she began. "Please don't close the door on me." I didn't move. "Can I come in just for a minute?" She sounded desperate.

I didn't answer; I just stepped back into the kitchen, leaving the door open behind me, trying to buy myself a little time to think. She came in and softly shut the door. We sat at the small table that had been in this apartment since we were girls. How many times had we sat here in the past, eating my beloved grandmother's delicacies? Many things in the apartment had changed since then, but at my grandmother's insistence, the tiny table- barely big enough for three- was still there. In this kitchen, the food was always fragrant and delicious, and conversation flowed easily. This was where I felt most at home, and although my grandparents have departed from this world, my mother still insists that the table remains where it is.

Tamari's face registered surprise when she saw the table: a piece of her history right before her eyes. She tried to capture my gaze, but I kept my eyes on the community garden outside. Pushing the hair from her face, she said she could hardly believe how little my grandmother's kitchen had changed. I turned to her, and our eyes met, and for a minute all I wanted was to fall onto her neck and sob endlessly. Perhaps that would alleviate some of my uneasiness.

Tamari asked how it felt to live in my grandparents' apartment, and I told her it was OK. In the beginning it was a little odd, mostly because they themselves were no longer there, but I got used to it. I think she was trying to ease the tension between us, but the ice wouldn't break. She had to find the courage, and the words, that had eluded her through our many years of separation.

"I don't know where to start," she said. I shrugged. "I came to ask for your forgiveness- that's what I was trying to tell you yesterday. I'm sorry for everything."

But I wasn't going to make this easy for her. I wanted an explanation. Stalling for time, I squirmed in my seat, trying unsuccessfully to find a comfortable position. Finally, I lifted my head and looked her straight in the eye. I could have drowned in those eyes that had been part of my life for so many years- longer than I'd lived with my husband.

"Tamari," I said, and paused. What did I stand to lose? I couldn't save our friendship, and I was trying to climb out of the quicksand that was about to swallow me up. And if I had nothing to lose, why should I help her find the right words?

"Look," I said, "your apology isn't the issue here. I don't think there's anything to say about what did and didn't happen."

"I think you deserve an apology," she insisted. "For all the years that I kept my distance, that I shut you out of my life even though you still played such an important role."

"What are you talking about?" All kinds of thoughts flashed through my head. Memories rose to the surface and enveloped me, and I was overcome with an intense, and familiar, feeling of embarrassment. I couldn't sit anymore; I got up and walked back to the small window overlooking the playground.

"I'm sorry," she repeated. "I'm sorry about all the years I didn't cherish you enough. I'm sorry that I was so heartless, and that I didn't reciprocate your generosity. I was so caught up in my own emotions- my anger, my sadness, my pain- that I didn't take the time to stop and think about you. All those years I thought my life was a living hell and yours was perfect. I know that wasn't realistic or true, that life isn't so black and white, but I would only let myself see my blackness and your whiteness. It was easier for me that way. But then I started envying you, then hating you. Please forgive me. I'm so ashamed of myself."

I didn't understand what she was trying to tell me, but the words "sorry" and "hate" were resonating in my brain. Confused, I turned to her. "What was there to hate me for? You thought my life was perfect, and I thought the same about yours, but I never hated you. All I felt was the pain of your abandonment, and a deep sense of shame."

She burst into tears. I walked over to her and started stroking her shoulder as if she was a sad and frustrated child, but she couldn't stop crying. At that point, perhaps I could have forgiven her, but what good would forgiveness do when we were separated by such a huge abyss? She sobbed for a long time; all I could do was pity her. I tried to understand what had prompted her to seek me out after all these years, but I couldn't. I didn't know what had happened in recent years that had led her to the realizations she had just shared with me. I felt sad and confused and nauseated, like my stomach was doing somersaults. I ran to the bathroom and vomited. By the time I returned to the kitchen, Tamari had pulled herself together.

"I don't understand," I said. "I don't understand why you looked for me and why you came here. What were you expecting, after all these years? That I would welcome you with open arms and everything would go back to being like it was? I don't have the energy I used to have," I added. "I'm tired and defeated and I have nothing left to give, not to you or anyone else."

She looked at me, astounded. "I didn't expect anything," she said, "really. It's just that I treated you badly, and you didn't deserve it. I am so sorry. And I've missed you terribly." When I didn't respond, she stood up, slipped her purse over her shoulder, and headed for the door. Then she tossed out, "I left Doron. I'm living in a rented apartment. Here's my phone number, if you want to get in touch." She scribbled the number on a piece of scrap paper and walked out, closing the door behind her. I sat there for a long time, nailed to my seat. I remembered different scenarios from our friendship, and the feeling of loneliness and humiliation that had been haunting me these past few years.

I remembered, painfully, Dan's withdrawal, and my alienation from my children, who were witnesses to my weakness. They didn't see me as "Supermom" anymore, able to solve all their problems. I was just me, an immigrant with faulty English and a heavy Israeli accent, pining away for her homeland, incapable of navigating her new country. That was the only reality they knew: a mother who couldn't help them with their homework, who avoided encounters with their teachers and their friends' parents. It was easier to keep her out of sight. Someone to sit at home, clean, cook, pick up after them- that was all they needed from a mother. They banned me from their lives almost entirely.

The pain was too much for me to bear. It made me want to run away. I was of no use to them, and they'd grown tired of my constant complaining and longing. My nerves were shot. In our last years together, I was jumping on them for every little thing; I could only reach them by attacking their lack of responsibility, their absent-mindedness. Instead of talking, I shouted. I shouted my pain, but I never put it into words. Instead of showing my wounds, I covered them up with screaming. I pounced on them all the time, for every tiny transgression. In the end, I felt that I had no choice but to leave them. It was the best thing for them, too. Otherwise I might lose them forever. My will to live was dwindling. I felt that nobody- besides myself- would love me, would comfort me.

Tamari's attempt at reconciliation was too little too late. In my current state of mind, I had no real use for her. I was tired and dejected, and I couldn't see any light in the horizon.

Slowly, I walked over to the phone, and dialed the crisis hotline. I'd had the number for a long time; now the time had come to use it. My life was no longer a life. In a quiet, toneless voice, I spoke. "I need help."

φφφ

When you fly into Seattle, right before you land, you see a giant mountain piercing the clouds: Mount Rainier. The significance of this mountain, its constant presence in the lives of Seattle's residents, is indisputable. It glistens all year long, and it makes you want to go there just to touch its sparkling, soothing whiteness. It is often veiled by clouds, but once it shakes them off, it takes your breath away.

My first day in Seattle, the sun was shining, and I had no idea that this was unusual. As we drove away from the airport, we saw Lake Washington stretching before us. The landscape was bathed in late-summer early-fall colors: different shades of reds, purples, oranges, and yellows. Yonatan was delighted by the foliage; he wanted to touch everything. I remember thinking how lucky I was to have come to this beautiful place with the two men in my life.

Life seemed hopeful and beautiful, and my heart was overflowing with love. I never would have guessed that one day it would all fall apart.

All this dazzling beauty, with all its grey days, made me sleepy. The days felt like nights, and the nights felt endless and disquieting. Autumn embraced winter, winter crept into spring, and green turned to gray.

It wasn't long before I ran up against real life. It took me a long time to learn how to deal with the loneliness. It was bleak, painful, biting. Dan was consumed by his work, and I was left alone to deal with daily life, completely unprepared for all the challenges that entailed. I think that's how it is for new immigrants, especially when their spouses are working.

My English was rudimentary at best. I had studied at the university, but all I read there were scholarly articles that had nothing to do with real life. They didn't teach me any of the basics: what the different parts of the body were called, or other necessities of life, or how various appliances worked. Everything was complicated, nothing was simple. I would often find myself stumbling over the most basic words. The frustration was awful, and it made me feel inferior to the person I was speaking with. Very slowly, I learned to plan my exact words before I even opened my mouth. The most fundamental questions left me feeling stupid and helpless, and there were all kinds of products with names I couldn't pronounce. Because of my accent, people were always asking me where I came from, which only intensified my feelings of foreignness and alienation. It's not that I was embarrassed by my homeland; it's just that I felt so cut off from everyone else. Most of the time, I felt like I had been unwillingly severed from the country I loved so deeply: I ached for it, I felt its pain… and I waited.

As I said, the holidays were particularly hard. This was when the loneliness was keener than ever. Whether we were alone or with other people, the emphasis on family only made me feel more out of place. Some of the holidays made me feel sick to my stomach: Halloween, for example, the holiday of the Christian saints, whom I associate with anti-Semitism and baseless hatred. And even though it made *me* think of pogroms, the children loved it. Every year, they couldn't wait to get dressed up and go trick-or-treating. I recoiled from the front lawns that were decorated like graveyards, and from the skeletons that hung in the windows, but the children adored the holiday, and I had no choice but to accompany them from house to house, knocking on doors, collecting candy- and making sure they were safe.

As Dan became more and more acclimated, I was drawn deeper into my children's lives. Their world became my world. And so it went, year after year. I missed Israel so much, it was physically painful.

Over time, I began to accept that Dan's promises to return to Israel were not going to be fulfilled. Dan didn't miss his old life, and to him, the advantages of our new life in America were enormous. He didn't even miss his family, as long as he could talk to them on the phone once a week and visit them once a year. They were so far away, and they didn't speak the language. The geographical distance seemed to be the biggest obstacle for his parents. As they aged, they found all kinds of excuses for why they couldn't come, and eventually we stopped inviting them. In any case, our connection to them was weaker than ever.

φφφ

The more Dan pulled away from me, the more I withdrew into myself. There were days I didn't even want to get out of bed and begin my daily routine, which I found dull and frustrating. One day looked just like the next, filled with grey skies and menial tasks. My only consolation, really, was food, and while it was a sweet comfort, it was also a harmful one. I searched for new and exotic dishes to fill my empty life. I baked, I cooked, and most of all, I ate. Within a few years, I had put on an unbelievable amount of weight. I was disgusted with myself, and yet I didn't do anything to change the situation. I continued to eat, and I continued to despise my appearance. Dan didn't care; as far as he was concerned, I could have been the fat lady of the circus. He wasn't bothered by my "plumpness." On the contrary, food was something we bonded over. Sometimes we cooked together, but mostly we ate together. Unlike me, though, Dan didn't put on any weight: he was addicted to physical activity, while I didn't venture out beyond my four walls.

In the United States, heavy people are not an uncommon sight. Many people struggle with their weight, and with the diseases that result from being overweight. Nonetheless, I couldn't get used to my new proportions, and I tried to hide my body under loose clothes. Then one day I heard Yonatan tell one of his friends that his mother was a big woman in every sense of the word. She had a big personality, a big heart, and a big body. He wasn't trying to hurt me, but hearing that comment shook me up. I tried all kinds of diets, but I couldn't stick with any of them.

Abigail was chubby, too, and when she entered puberty, she began to starve herself. Maybe it was because of my own size. I didn't notice it right away. I didn't notice that the food on her plate remained untouched, or that whenever I gave her something to eat, she would throw it in the trash. I had no idea what she ate for lunch, since she had that meal at school. Her clothes hung loosely on her body, and whenever I brought it up, she retorted, "Not everybody has to be fat like you." Then she would apologize, and tell me she didn't mean what she said.

The fatter I got, the skinnier she got, and the more distant. When I asked her about her day, or about her teachers and friends, she would give me a one-word answer, then go back to whatever she was doing. As Yonatan got older, he didn't think too highly of me, either. Maybe this was a normal part of adolescence, maybe it happened in every family, but I was profoundly hurt and embarrassed that my children no longer wanted to spend time with me. I had done so much for them- why were they drifting further and further away?

November 22, 1994

Seattle

Dear Tamari,

I hope all is well. I tried calling as soon as I got your letter, but I couldn't get through, so I'm writing instead. I hope this letter reaches you. Soon you'll be having another baby, and this should be a time of joy, not sorrow.

You write about all the complications of pregnancy, and of life, and the only thing I can say to you is this: Were it not for my children, who make my life so full, I don't know what I'd do. You're telling me how scared you are of the additional responsibility, and meanwhile, here I am praying for another child. You tell me that Doron was thrilled to find out about your pregnancy, and all I can think of is how I wish Dan felt the same way. As you can see, everything is backwards.

I have no doubt that it will all work out: you'll be fine, and so will the baby, and your little family, and work... in other words, everything. You worry too much; just try to enjoy life.

Things here are fine, too. The children are sweet, and Dan is working very long hours. With all the chaos, I'm having trouble carving out some space for myself, and I spend most of my time looking after the needs and desires of my loved ones. Like you, I wonder if this is the lot of every mother and wife- to take care of everyone- and the answer seems to be yes. Still, I enjoy it, whereas you find the whole thing terrifying.

I'm trying to give you encouragement, but I'm not sure I'm succeeding, maybe because it's so late and I'm exhausted. The children fell asleep just a little while ago- Dan got home late, and they wanted to see him- so I'm wiped out.

Tomorrow we're supposed to go to the Oregon coast. It's Thanksgiving here, and as usual, we're taking every opportunity to see the country. There's another, more personal reason: I hate being here for the holidays. All around me, families are getting together, while here I am, so far away from my loved ones, and it's hard. It's supposed to be cold and rainy in Oregon, too, but perhaps a change of scenery will do us good. The kids are excited, and I'm busy packing. In the morning, we'll all pile into the car and head out. We rented a beach house for the weekend, and I won't have much cooking or cleaning to do because on vacation we go out to eat. The kids packed their own bags- they must think we're going away for a whole year: games and dolls of every shape and size, along with workbooks that I brought back from Israel. I'll tell you all about it when I get back.

In the meantime, hang in there, and remember: everything's going to be alright.

Love, Michal

2005

Over the years, my friendship with Tamari went through many stages. From our childhood friendship, when we shared every detail of our lives, to our army service, when the fabric of our friendship first started to unravel. I think we were at our closest when we traveled through Europe together. On that month-long trip, everything was programmed: we woke up together and went to sleep together. There was no time off, and no physical distance between us. Sometimes, when two people spend all their time together, it can feel like a pressure cooker, but for us, it was different. Our tastes, our desires, our interests- we were perfectly suited for each other. I couldn't have hoped for a better traveling companion. Our days were filled with exploring, our nights with heartfelt conversations. We had no obligations towards anyone else in the world, or to the world itself; the two of us were completely free. Tamari was so different from me; it was like she completed me. We laughed about everything and made plans for our next trip, which never came to pass. I met Dan, she met Doron, and our men simply didn't speak the same language. Our financial situations were different, too, and we were so far apart, both physically and- as a result- mentally.

How I missed those lovely moments….Tamari was the best friend I ever had. She was the only person I could really open up with. I depended on her in a way I had never depended on anyone else, which is why the breakdown in our relationship hurt me so deeply. I was alone for a long time: alone within my nuclear family, alone within my extended family, alone within my community, and alone in the rift between Tamari and me.

We never did get the money back. At some point, Dan and I resigned ourselves to the fact that the money would never be returned, and we put the whole episode behind us.

I had gotten myself tangled up in an unfeasible situation, and now I was ready to break out of it. I desperately missed my children, and I didn't know if I would ever be able to undo what had already been done. Would they forgive me for abandoning them? Would they understand that I had no choice? I was choosing between life and death, between wakefulness and endless sleep. between explosive outbursts and long periods without communication-something that didn't help anyone, and only alienated them more. I didn't love myself, and I didn't think I was worthy of their love. I believed that they were better off without me, and I without them. The only thing that connected us was pain, and I couldn't stand it any longer. After years of unabated frustration, I decided to do the unthinkable: I got up and left. I walked away from my home and my children. And as I climbed into the taxi that would take me to the airport, I didn't look back, not even for a second.

January 1, 1995

Seattle

Happy New Year! It's a new secular year, full of hopes and dreams. I don't usually celebrate New Year's Day, but yesterday was different. We were invited to a party for Dan's work, and even though I didn't want to, he begged me to go with him, so I finally agreed. How bad could it be? Well, surprisingly- and for a change- I actually enjoyed myself. It was an elegant party in one of Seattle's fanciest hotels. I bought myself an evening gown and high heels (OK, not exactly high, but high enough to make me look a little more feminine), and Dan even wore a sport jacket. I felt like I was in Hollywood. It was fun to look on from the sidelines and observe all the stylish clothes, all the glamour and beauty that filled the room. It's an experience every woman should have once in her lifetime: to be Cinderella at the ball.

In one room, they were handing out cigars. Somehow I managed to sneak in and smoke my first Cuban cigar! I felt like a little like a gangster, which made me laugh. Dan brought me a glass of whiskey, and for a few minutes I didn't have a care in the world.

I woke up the next morning to a pounding headache and a party in my bed. When I started telling the kids about the gala, Yonatan got up and left, but Abigail stayed in my bed, wrapped in my arms. Over and over again, I described everything I had seen and heard and experienced. What fun it can be, belonging to the world of girls! When we finished talking, we went out for breakfast together.

Half an hour later, Dan went to meet some friends, and I went back to my regular life. I took the kids to the movies, and now I'm home. It's late already, and Dan's still not back. I tried calling him, but he's not picking up. I can't help wondering where he is and what he's doing. Does this ever happen to you that Doron disappears and you can't get in touch with him? As a rule, I try not to ask him where he was. It just makes him angry, and why go looking for a fight?

Love, me

2005

After a fitful night, I woke up drenched in sunshine. Not only had I not close the blinds, but I'd left the windows open, too. I wanted the cold air to flow into my room and penetrate my bones, hoping that it might rouse my sluggish body and soul. It was early in the morning, the day was clear, and the sunshine warmed my frozen body. I lay there, perfectly still, closing my tired eyes, surrendering my face to the sun that slowly thawed my bones and warmed my aching heart.

I had spent most of my money, and I missed my children more than ever. The conversation I had a couple of days ago with the support counselor had ignited a spark of hope: perhaps all wasn't lost. She gave me the name of a therapist, and I decided to make an appointment.

Tamari's visit had confused me. Should I let her back into my life? Would I ever be able to trust her affection? Or even to ask her for help? All kinds of thoughts swirled through my head and left me in a state of turmoil. I tried to put them in order, to find a way out. Everything was so complicated; the obstacles seemed insurmountable. I tried to put aside my emotions and to focus on finding a solution. It was time for me to stop torturing myself and to start enjoying my life for what it was. Maybe I could finally give hope a chance to blossom; maybe I could finally live.

More than anything, I wanted the pain to go away, the pain that had been burrowing deeper and deeper into in my heart. This time, I was going to try to befriend the pain. At first I found this idea preposterous, but I was trying to think out of the box, to come up with a new approach. If the pain was already there, I might as well try warming up to it; maybe then it would stop hurting so much. The pain wasn't going away any time soon; perhaps the best thing to do would be to make peace with it, until one day it would finally disappear and never come back.

The first thing to do, I told myself, was to get up and make the bed, something I hadn't done in months, figuring that I was the only one sleeping in that room. I stood up, straightened the sheets, and went into the shower. When I looked in the mirror, I saw a tired face and a headful of unkempt, grey hair. I couldn't remember the last time I'd washed it.

I lay down in the bathtub, the same tub that my grandparents had used, that I had used when I was a little girl, as far back as I can remember. It made me smile. I let the water wash over my body; perhaps it was cleansing my soul as well. I lay there for a long time. At one point I thought I heard a tune being hummed; then I realized it was coming from me. Afterwards, when I looked in the mirror again, I noticed that I had lost some weight. I always wear the same black pants, and I rotate between a few shirts, so it was hard to tell. I smiled at my reflection, then left the bathroom.

I made myself a cup of coffee, and carried it over to the kitchen window overlooking a small park. I watched the people coming and going, rushing off to work. An elderly couple was sitting on a bench in the sun. The woman's arms were wrapped around the man. They sat and talked amicably; it looked like nothing could cast a shadow on their morning. I envied their companionship and their serenity, and I wondered if I would ever find someone to love, someone who would truly love me. Resisting the urge to climb back into bed, I continued to stand there, looking out at the garden. When I had recovered, I decided the time had come to venture out into life instead of just watching it. I hadn't left my family and come all the way to Tel Aviv just so I could gaze upon life from the outside.

I'd have to resolve the financial situation quickly: I'd look for a job in my field. Maybe I'd get in touch with the office I worked for years ago. I didn't know where to begin. I had nobody to consult with. I felt utterly alone, like there was nobody in the whole world who I could talk to. I had lost both my parents, and Tamari- my only friend- was now a part of my past. I certainly couldn't count on my brothers, who objected to every decision I ever made.

I walked over to the phone and dialed the number the counselor had given me. The voice on the other end of the line was pleasant. We made an appointment for the following afternoon; I still had a day and a half until then. Maybe I'd go to Tel Aviv and pay a visit to the occupational therapy clinic I used to work at; I had some connections there.

φφφ

I didn't recognize a single person at the clinic, and I was told there were no openings. It's not that I had such high hopes, but I also wasn't expecting that all my co-workers would be gone. It seems that when the salaries are low, nobody stays. Or so they told me. After I left, I strolled through the streets, waiting for them to draw me in. The streets are a good antidote for my loneliness. On the one hand, those strolls make me miss my children even more-especially when I pass an ice cream shop, a music store, or the beach, anywhere kids their age like to hang out. On the other hand, all the commotion on the streets reminds me that there are homes with a mother, a father, family, noise, joy, chaos, shouting... there is life!

I never imagined that I would go for months at a time without hearing my children's voices or seeing their faces. Had I made a mistake?

This wasn't the first time I'd asked myself this question, and it wouldn't be the last. Every day I torment myself with these thoughts; they close in on me, they smother me. My beloved Yonatan and Abigail, how sweet they were in their infancy, and in their later years, too. And how painful it was to discover one day that they no longer needed me. My time had passed, I thought, my offerings have been rejected, and I almost sunk back into the bitterness I knew so well, but this time I tried to look at things a little differently. The most important thing was to ward off that suffocating feeling that had been persecuting me every day.

214

I left my kids, and they're still OK. That's what I told myself. I knew I could always count on Dan to take good care of them. Although back in the States, I never left their side, I often felt like the three of them were shutting me out of their personal space, like I was standing on the sidelines, looking on as the three of them grew closer and closer. I felt like I didn't belong.

I had given everything I had, even more than everything, until I had nothing left to give.

I ducked into a café and ordered a glass of fresh-squeezed orange juice. I sat with my back to the wall and looked out the window at the passers-by, remembering the times when all I wanted was to belong. To belong to the family I came from, to belong to the family I had created, to belong to my friendship with Tamari, to belong to *something*. And then I suddenly realized that the one kind of belonging I had never thought about was the feeling of belonging to my native land.

I had let people down, or they had let me down, but my homeland had never disappointed me. The sea is still the same sea, the mountains the same mountains. The Sea of Galilee is as it always was, and the Galil, and the desert, and my beloved and familiar vistas- they will always be what they always were. A sense of serenity flowed through my whole body, and I smiled. What I needed most was right here; all that was left for me to do was accept whatever treasures it had to offer.

I continued to walk until I finally got to the beach. I bought myself an ice cream cone: chocolate-vanilla, the flavors of childhood. I licked the cone off the sides to keep the ice cream from dripping onto my clothes. Within two minutes, it was gone, and my smile grew even broader. Then I went home and fell into a deep, dreamless sleep that- at least for a few hours- saved me from myself.

When I woke up, it was already dark. The air was cold. I wrapped myself in my blanket and listened to the sounds of the house as it welcomed me into its company. I checked the clock: it was almost nine. I walked into the kitchen, picked up the phone, and called Tamari.

February 12, 1995

Tel Aviv

Hey Michal,

How's it going? My sweet little Tomer is already almost a month old. He's a good boy, and he tries to make his mother's life as easy as possible. He wakes up to eat every three hours, but other than that, he's a good sleeper. It wasn't like that with Lianni, whose stomach was always bothering her. I don't sleep much at night, but I suppose that's normal. I keep telling Doron that it's time for us to move. Our apartment is tiny, you can hardly breathe, especially now that we have two kids. Doron wants to start his own business, so I'm not sure this apartment thing is going to work out, but we'll see what happens after his business gets underway.

As you know, I have a hard time with newborns. The fatigue takes its toll on me, and breastfeeding makes me feel like a cow. Fortunately, nobody got on my case this time around, except for one of the nurses who kept shooting me dirty looks whenever I took out a bottle. Doron helps with the last feeding of the day, and that gives me about four hours of uninterrupted sleep. It's not much, but I need it, and my children need a mother who is calm. I try my best to be patient and even-tempered, but I don't always succeed. The bottom line is, things are complicated.

Our mothers help us out every afternoon, after Lianne comes home. It's a lifesaver, because Doron doesn't get home until very late. Lianni is so proud of her little brother; she must think he's a toy. She pulls his ears and his hands, and then gets very upset when he starts to cry. I can't leave her alone with him for a minute, even if he's in his bouncy seat or his crib. She always finds a way to reach him and pull something. I don't see any signs of jealousy yet, but I'm sure that will come, too.

I don't know how I'll ever go back to work with two little ones at home, but you know me, staying home makes me lose my mind, not to mention the fact that, as usual, we really need the money. If we do decide to buy a place, do you think you might be able to help us out with a loan? Doron and I will get in touch with you to talk about the details. We're thinking about buying a bigger house, but we're $100,000 short. We can't take out a mortgage, but we promise to return the money we borrowed as soon as we can, definitely within a year or so. After that, we can pay the rest back in monthly increments. Your help would truly save us, and we would be so grateful. You know how much I love you, and you know you can count on us.

I love you very much.

Hope to see you soon,

Yours,

Tamari

April 21, 1995

Tamari,

Another Passover outside of Israel, A week before the holiday, I discovered that everyone else but me had already made plans for the Seder. We hadn't invited any of our friends, and none of them had invited us; we were going to celebrate alone. True, one of Dan's colleagues had invited us, but I didn't want to spend the Seder with people I'd never even met, so it ended up being just us. It was the saddest holiday ever.

Judaism means nothing to Dan, but for me, it's a link that can't be broken, the only thing that gives me a sense of belonging. I bought the kids activity books about the holidays, and little Haggadot for the Seder, which they held for all of twenty minutes. In the end, we only made it through a few pages before eating dinner. Afterwards, I was the only one left at the table. This time, I decided, I would read every word of the entire Haggadah, including all the songs. And so it was. I read, I sang, I cried... and there was nobody there to dry my tears, because I wouldn't let anyone see me crying. And anyway, I was the only one here with a connection to Israel and Judaism. Everyone else is completely uninterested in these Pagan rituals, so I had no reason to expect any sympathy.

When I finished singing, I cleared the table, washed the dishes, and called my mother to see how their Seder was. She told me how they all celebrated together, and I could feel my heart turning sour.

I was trying to keep bread and other leavened food- out of the house, but Dan took the kids to an arcade, followed by pizza. I was furious. His response was that when I took the kids out, I could do what I wanted, but when the kids were with him, I couldn't tell him what he could or couldn't do. Sometimes I almost hate him for ignoring my feelings and my wishes, and I wonder how we got to this point, and I have no answers. That makes me even more desperate, and I start to ask all kinds of unanswerable questions.

Thank you for understanding me and for being there for me. It's the best gift you can give me.

The day after the Seder didn't feel like a holiday. Everything went on as usual. Here, if you're looking for a festive atmosphere, you have to go to synagogue, something I've never particularly enjoyed. In Israel everything connected to the holidays- Shabbat celebrations, memorial days- and the knowledge that whether or not you observe the Jewish rituals, is just there. You don't even have to go to Synagogue; you are surrounded by the holiday atmosphere. It's a part of me. And I want it to be a part of my children, too, although they're growing up in the Diaspora and are American through and through. I fight for every shred of Israeli identity. I try to enforce a strictly-Hebrew policy at home, but the kids speak English to each other. English is their primary language; they spend most of their day speaking English, and at night, it is the language of their dreams. Hebrew is an invasive plant, nothing more than a headache. Dan isn't bothered by this at all. He talks to them in English, and he doesn't seem the slightest bit troubled by the fact that they're drifting further and further away from Israeli culture. And if I'm the only one who cares, does that make me the problem?

How are you getting along? I hope our loan will help you get a bigger apartment.

Please let me know what's going on with you, and what it was like to go back to work. And please send my love to Doron.

Kisses,

Michal

2005

After the third ring I heard her voice, so familiar to me. I could feel my heart breaking. My eyes filled with tears, and I couldn't make a sound. Tamari asked who was calling, and after a few long seconds, I responded.

"Tamari, it's me."

"Hi," she said. "I'm so happy to hear your voice." I smiled through the tears, thinking how both our lives have undergone such radical changes. I had to resist the maternal urge to take on her pain, as I had done for so many years.

"It wasn't easy, calling you," I confessed.

"But I'm glad you did. I miss our friendship."

That last sentence stunned me. I didn't say a word, but a jumble of thoughts popped into my head. What exactly was it that she missed?

I couldn't hold back.

"What was it, exactly, that you missed about our friendship?"

Her response surprised me, the part where we talk. About anything, it doesn't matter what.

I smiled, trying not to let my bitterness taint these moments of grace.

"Yes, it really has been a long time since we've talked."

"I missed you. I'm sorry I pushed you away," she said, and I realized how much I've needed her these past few years, how lonely I've been, and I almost succumbed to the emotions that were washing over me.

"Why did you do it? We were so close…." My voice, barely more than a whisper, got caught in my throat.

"At first it was because I was so busy with the kids and with Doron and with our never-ending financial problems, and with life itself, and I felt like you were living in Hollywood over there. Sure, part of you wanted to come back, but it was like you were living on Mount Olympus looking down on us from above. I felt like I had nothing to contribute to our friendship. Look where you were and look where I was!"

"That's funny," I said, feeling the bitterness inside me trying to escape. "Which Olympus are you talking about, exactly? You were here, surrounded by family, getting all the help you needed, while I was there, at the end of the world, alone, utterly alone. Do you have any idea what it feels like to be completely alone?"

She paused for a few seconds; she must have been trying to think of an appropriate response. Then she spoke:

"Loneliness, in my opinion, is something that exists in all of us; sometimes I feel lonely, too. But I don't think I really understand what you're describing."

I appreciated her honesty. She didn't reprimand me or contradict me; she just gave me space to feel what I felt. She didn't turn it into a competition over which one of us was the lonelier of the two. For a minute I felt those old feelings of closeness coming back. One of the strengths of our friendship was that we respected each other's space, and we validated every feeling, no matter how strange it might be. That had never happened in any other friendship in my entire life. We were quiet for a minute; then she spoke.

"Let's meet for coffee," she suggested." I know it's late, but this is the best time of day for me. The little one is sleeping, and I can tell Lianni that I'm going out. We can meet at 'The Bookworm.' What do you say?"

I didn't have anything better to do, and I knew that after taking such a long afternoon nap, I wouldn't be able to fall asleep, anyway.

"OK," I said. "Give me fifteen minutes."

φφφ

For the first few years in the United States, I tried to cultivate friendships with women my age. The easiest thing was to socialize with women whose kids were the same age as mine. All the women were young, well-educated, and- because they couldn't get a work visa- bored to tears. We called our group "The Joy of Motherhood." All of us had had successful careers in Israel, before we moved here with our husbands. Everyone had at least a bachelor's degree; many of us had gone to graduate school. There were even two women who had just completed their doctorates. They had gone from being busy, successful career women to frustrated housewives.

In general, after a couple of years, they would realize that they needed to find a new occupation. Some of them went back to school, some of them were artists of one kind or another; the important thing was to keep their minds and their souls busy, to break away from their humdrum American lives.

The mornings were endless. Those of us with small kids were hostages to our children's schedules. Only the mothers whose children were already in pre-school could find the time to do something for themselves.

In our area, the expectation was that once women had children, they would stop working so they could stay home with their kids. It wasn't just the Israelis; the American women did this, too. They had knitting circles, play groups, all kinds of activities that served two purposes: to get the kids together, and to give the mothers an opportunity to get out of the house and socialize. Young mothers who stayed home with their kids were given a lot of support. The phrase we heard most often was "your hands are full." American society recognized the importance of taking care of children, and these mothers were treated with respect. Back in Israel, some of my friends had stayed home to raise their children, but people tended to look down on them. Most of these women were financially secure, and maybe the comments people made were rooted in jealousy. People were always asking them, "What do you do all day?" As if childcare wasn't the equivalent of several full-time jobs combined. It is important, exhausting, draining work, with no prestige and very little recognition.

I threw my lot in with my fellow moms. It was nice for a while. Once or twice a week, we'd get together with our kids. But when my children started school, we lost touch. Most of my friends went back to Israel, a handful stayed in the United States, and of those people, only a few stayed in Seattle. The whole time we were there, women came and went, more coming than going. It felt a little like a train station, the population always changing.

At one point, I started distancing myself from the other Israelis. I didn't like all the gossip and the intrusiveness, and I couldn't stop yearning for Israel. All I could think about was how much I wanted to go back; most of the women felt the way I did. It was strange, how the women all missed Israel, while most of the men had no desire to go back. I think the high taxes, the difficulty of making a living, the many days, randomly distributed, of reserve duty, the lack of leisure time- all these things reinforced their reluctance to return to Israel. I knew quite a few couples who fought over this issue. In the end, most of them gave in to their spouses and went back. Sometimes, after a few years, the arguing would stop. They got used to life in America; their grown children didn't want to move to a place they associated with vacations, and grandparents, and aunts and uncles, and hanging out at the beach; the parents had fewer responsibilities and were ready to relax and have fun. That's what happened with my kids, too, only I never got used to living in the States, and my husband pulled away from me, and when my kids grew up, they pulled away, too, and I lost so much that in the end, I had nothing left to lose.

July 25, 1995

Seattle

Hey Tamari,

Haven't heard from you in a while. I tried calling you a few times, but nobody picked up, not even your secretary, so I couldn't leave a message. Here, the school year is over, and the kids are out for the summer. Yonatan will be starting first grade. I never imagined that we would still be here, that Yonatan would be going to first grade in America, that my mother wouldn't be able to walk him to school, that his classes would be taught in English and not Hebrew. Once again, I asked Dan about moving back to Israel, and he promised me that we could go back in another two or three years. He wants to save up enough money for us to buy a house with a garden. It's true, I would like that- a house with fruit trees and a dog and a cat- but waiting another few years? It's difficult, and it's complicated. Thankfully, Abigail is still home with me, cheering me up, making me smile. She is all sweetness and joy- she's just a delight. I love dressing her up in girly clothes, lots of pink. She's already talking in full sentences. You would like her.

What are your plans for the summer? It rained almost every day in June. In the beginning of July, the sun graced us with its presence for a few days before disappearing again. I can't wait for the sun to warm up my face and my body. Most days are overcast; on sunny days, I try to take my kids to the lake. We might visit to the eastern part of the state. There's a dam there that's one of the biggest in the world, and at night they put on a sound and light show about how it was built. Sounds interesting. I wish you could come, too. Maybe next year....

Dan asked me to remind you that the first payment of your loan is due next month. Please don't forget to transfer the money on time, as our mortgage payments are also due in the beginning of the month, and if your payment is late, we'll have to borrow money from our other accounts. Here in America, they're sticklers about getting your payments in on time. In fact, even one late payment can mess up your credit rating, which can cause a lot of problems down the line. So please don't forget.

What's new with you? Drop me a line.

Love,

Michal

φφφ

Before I went to meet her, I tried to think about what I was going to say. It was strange: was I really letting her back into my life? Could I trust her this time? In the end, I decided I really had nothing to lose. I promised myself that I would never let her hurt me again. I know how to dress myself with a suit of armor (or do I? Maybe not....). I decided I would just listen to her; that made it easier. I found a thin cotton tunic that I liked- it felt like someone was hugging me- and I draped it over my shoulders. With my arms crossed in an attempt to exude confidence, I headed towards the café.

It was getting on towards evening, and it was lovely. Although there was no breeze, it wasn't too hot. People were walking past me, but I was so caught up in my memories of our shared childhood, I didn't even see them. When I got to the café, Tamari was already there, sitting by the window. She saw me right away, and broke into a smile. I went in and sat across from her.

She looked both happy and embarrassed. "Thanks for coming," she said.

I was silent for a moment. "The truth is," I finally said, "I had nothing better to do." As soon as those awful words were out of my mouth, I wanted to take them back. "I'm also glad I came," I added, trying to repair the damage.

There we sat, two grown women in their mid-forties, each of us carrying a heavy, painful load. I felt like a complete failure, and while I didn't know exactly what she was feeling, my sense was that she wasn't too pleased with herself, either.

It was a little like old times, albeit without the giggling. This was a much more serious conversation, and it felt more honest, too. Tamari herself seemed more truthful, and so did the things we said. I learned about what had happened over the years after we lost touch, things I never knew. I listened more than I spoke. It had been a long time since I'd sat down with someone close to me and heard about that person's life.

It hadn't been easy for Tamari. Years without a reliable income, a lack of financial and emotional stability, three young children (they had a third child, I learned), relatives who were always arguing over which one of them would help out with the kids or money, and barely acknowledging how hard it was for Tamari just going through the day. She talked about how she had been chronically tired for years, how her demanding job and her difficult relationship with Doron had taken their toll on her. She worked two full shifts- one at her job, the other at home- while Doron sat around doing nothing. He had been severely depressed and unable to function. She tried to help him, to stand by him, but he pushed her away. And so both of them dug their heels into their own anger, until they finally decided to dismantle what they had built. This all happened a year ago. He was still her friend, she said, but not a close one.

Her career had taken off, and she was now in charge of several major accounts. The kids were sweet; maybe I'd like to meet them. She hoped that we could go back to being close friends, because although she had more than enough friends, she only felt like herself when she was with me.

I felt sorry for her. I tried to be understanding, but I didn't want to go back to always being the supportive one. Tamari had a habit of getting herself into all kinds of difficult situations, and relying on other people to bale her out. I hoped she had matured. Perhaps she'd started taking some responsibility for her life; I couldn't be sure. There was no doubt in my mind that I needed a friend to listen to me, maybe to help me see things differently. Someone who could help me climb out of the muck that was my life. Was she the one? I wasn't ready to pour out my heart to her, not yet, and I found myself listening in almost complete silence. When she was done, I felt like she was parachuting into the same black holes I knew so well, and that my job was to go and rescue her.

At the end of the evening, we said goodbye. Neither of us had committed to anything. I didn't want to be indebted to her, and I still wasn't sure I could trust her. I felt like the abyss between us was all that remained.

φφφ

In my last year in Seattle, I could barely function. My sense of despondency was overwhelming, and there was no respite. I could feel my life getting smaller every day. My husband and children were completely baffled by my desire to return to Israel, and my dream of moving back with my family was vanishing into thin air. It was clear to me that I could never have the life I wanted. Aside from the births of my children, all my dreams felt out of reach. I lived a stunted life, and even as my body grew, my emotions disappeared. Dan didn't notice- by then, we were rarely intimate; he didn't say anything, and neither did I. This arrangement worked for both of us, for different reasons. The children who'd kept me so busy all those years were now occupied with their own interests, and I felt like I had turned into a liability.

Yes, I drove the kids around, did the shopping, met with the teachers, took them to the doctors, made sure they were happy and healthy. I was there for them, both behind the scenes and center-stage. But as the years passed, all of these jobs became less important. My children grew more independent, and started keeping their distance. And me? I could hardly even get out of bed in the morning. I spent endless hours watching TV and sitting in front of the computer, following the stories of people I didn't know who lived in places I've never seen and never will see. I didn't have a single soul to confide in. I didn't have any close friends. The truth is, I hadn't made much of an effort to make friends, and when people tried to get close to me, I retreated into myself. I wasn't interested in anything or anyone, other than my children, who seemed to grasp my unhappiness but were too young to process it. I was sure that they couldn't handle me, and my pain, and I didn't blame them. That's the way of the world: there's a mother and a father who give everything they can to their children, and then there are the children, who take from their parents but don't want to- or don't know how to- give back, partly because nobody ever asked them for anything.

The more dejected I felt, the fewer solutions there seemed to be. My hasty flight to Israel was a desperate measure, something I hadn't planned or foreseen. The fact that my grandparents' apartment had just been vacated weeks before, not long enough to have found a new tenant, was an incentive to move quickly. It meant that I had somewhere to go, a place to rest my head.

I was very tired, and I didn't think about the fact that no matter where I went, I would bring myself with me, or that there's no such thing as a quick fix.

The following morning brought a pleasant breeze. I stretched my entire body and looked out the window on a clear blue sky, extending as far as the eye could see. A memory of the previous night passed through my head briefly, lightly, as if it had left only the faintest mark. I went over my conversation with Tamari, trying to remember how it had made me feel. I came to the conclusion that whatever I'd felt hadn't been too powerful: it wasn't sorrow, or anger, or frustration. It was as if I hadn't really been there. Maybe, I thought, this was simply a new defense mechanism to help me deal with unpleasant circumstances, but I couldn't be sure. I decided to put an end to this dime-store analysis of myself, and to get out of bed immediately. It was time for a change, I thought; then I burst out laughing. It seems I only made changes after I had exhausted all my other options, and here I was again, about to make a change.

Someone to talk to. That much was clear: what I needed was someone to talk to, even if I had to pay for it. Someone who would finally listen to me. I had always kept quiet, whether I was with Dan and the children or inside my grandparents' apartment.

I was glad I had contacted the crisis hotline, and that I'd made an appointment with Ronit, the psychologist. From our brief phone conversation, I'd gotten the sense that she was the right person for me. I wanted a female therapist, and someone who lived nearby. A woman could understand me better, I thought, and I wanted to be able to see her without too much effort. I had made the appointment with Ronit both because the hotline recommended her, and because the way she paused between words gave me room for my own words. The following morning, I showed up for the scheduled appointment.

I told her about myself, although I didn't go into detail: after all, I didn't really know her. She didn't say much. Mostly she nodded her head to show that she was listening. I told her, in a general way, about my friendship with Tamari and about my children, who were so far away, and she responded with a single short sentence. I don't remember her exact words, but it was something to the effect of, "Living far from your children is like having one of your limbs torn off, isn't it?" I thought this was a somewhat odd response. Did she think I was going to agree with her? Argue with her? Why had she asked that question? After exactly fifty minutes, she asked me if I wanted to meet with her again. I said yes; what did I have to lose, besides money? And I didn't have anyone else to talk to. With Ronit, I could finally talk about my mixed-up life, and she would listen.

After I left the clinic, I walked back to my favorite bookstore in town. I was looking for an easy read, thinking about how it had been several hours since I'd last checked in on my neighbors. I hadn't been keeping track of who had come back, and when. I hadn't even looked out at the playground to see if Roni and Dafna were there with their little one. It felt strange to be in this lovely bookstore, to think that there was life outside of my little Tel Aviv apartment. A sharp pain pierced my heart. My children, my beloved children. A yearning, so sharp it was almost intolerable, washed over me, and my eyes filled with tears. I wiped them away with my hand and went over to the Israeli literature section. I selected a book, ordered a cup of coffee, and sat down in a corner of the shop. I hadn't even finished the first page when I heard a familiar voice behind me: "Michal? Michal Cohen?"

I turned around, and there was D'vir. His tunic had been replaced by a pair of khakis, and his t-shirt by a button-down shirt. His long hair had been cut, revealing a small patch of baldness in his salt-and-pepper hair. It was hard to see the old D'vir in this man, but his voice was the same, and so were his eyes, despite the tiny wrinkles at their corners. I couldn't believe he had recognized me. And I was glad to see a familiar face. As for the fact that that face belonged to D'vir... I had mixed feelings about that.

He asked if he could join me, and I said yes. A couple of minutes later, we were deep into a lively conversation about the past, about what we had done then and what we were doing now. D'vir was a professor of philosophy at Haifa University, but he taught in Tel Aviv, too, and he came here one day a week. Stopping at "The

Bookworm" was part of his routine; he would schedule meetings here, or buy a book to read on his way home. When he said "home," my heart froze for a minute as I was besieged by thoughts of "What would have happened if...." I pushed those thoughts out of my mind, and suddenly I heard myself talking. Really talking. About myself. About all the things I couldn't bring myself to tell the psychologist; after all, she had only known me for all of fifty minutes, while D'vir had known me for years, and known me very well.

It felt so natural to sit across from him and tell him about myself, and suddenly I found myself thinking about all the years he had been missing from my life, and what I thought he had been doing with his life, and what he had actually been doing. I thought about how no matter what our dreams are; we never know how our lives will turn out. About how life takes us places we never even imagined, both physically and mentally. Who would have thought I would make my way to Seattle and live there for so many years? Who would have guessed I wouldn't be working in the field I had trained for so intensively?

Who would have thought that I would turn into a lonely, frustrated housewife? That I would leave my husband and children and go back to Israel, alone? Or that I would be an orphan by the age of forty? Who would have believed that I would be so lonely, and that Tamari would no longer be my dearest friend? Who would have guessed? Who would have guessed that I'd be sitting in this bookstore across from a forty-plus balding man with a brilliant smile and kind eyes? Who would have thought I'd suddenly feel worthy?

I felt that way because D'vir was interested in me. In *me*. Not in what kind of mother I was or what kind of wife or daughter or girlfriend, but in *me*. In Michal. The woman he had loved, the woman who had left him, then left her husband and her children. The woman who might have been a serial leaver, from whom any reasonable man would keep his distance?

I tried not to surrender to these troubling thoughts, not to fall back into the abyss. I continued with my story; I couldn't stop talking, and D'vir didn't try to stem the rushing current of words that were streaming from my mouth. He just listened. And suddenly I was able to talk about my childhood without tearing up, and about Dan, and the beautiful city of Seattle, and the last few excruciating years. In the middle of this conversation- in which I spoke and he listened- I suddenly realized that I was no longer waiting for Dan, no longer waiting for him to give me permission to speak to my kids or to allow them to visit me. I am their mother, just as much as he is their father. True, he wasn't the one to walk out on them, but he also had never really been there for them. I raised them, and I love them, and I always will. This sudden realization made me stop mid-speech. I remained quiet and allowed myself to be swept into daydreams of me hugging my children to my chest, of my children running towards me in the airport. For a few seconds, I even felt joy. Then I dove back into D'vir's eyes, and that's when I realized that he had taken my hand in his, as if he were part of the fantasy.

I didn't pull my hand away, but I averted my gaze. For the first time in a long time, I felt the warmth of human touch with all its many powers: the power to envelop, to lighten one's load, to ease the exhausting pangs of a guilty conscience. My eyes filled with tears; very gently, he wiped them away. He asked me to continue, and I went on with my story. Mostly I talked about my children. When he stopped me to ask their ages, and I said one was almost seventeen and one was almost fourteen, I realized how old they were, and how young. I hoped I hadn't destroyed their lives. I thought about the fact that while I had chosen to live in Tel Aviv these last few months, I hadn't really been living. For a moment I wondered if I was neglecting my neighbors; for the second day in a row, I had no idea what they were doing, when they were leaving, when they were coming home. I felt a momentary relief, mingled with guilt, and once again, I felt terribly confused. I slid my hand out of D'vir's; I had to stop being so selfish, I thought. I couldn't reel him in to the disaster that was me.

D'vir didn't seem bothered when I pulled my hand away. He asked me what I was doing in Tel Aviv. Was I visiting? That's when I realized that I still hadn't told him about my abandonment. I was afraid that if I told him, he would run away, so I kept silent.

"Are you on vacation?" he ventured.

"Sort of," I answered, then directed the conversation back to him. I asked him about all the years that had passed, when I knew nothing about him other than the fact that he was married and had a daughter.

"What can I tell you?" he replied. "I studied in Haifa, I got married, I had a daughter, Noga, who's now ten. My wife and I didn't get along very well, and three years ago we got divorced, but we're still friends. Noga is the most important thing in my life. It's because of her that I never stay over in Tel Aviv, why I'm always in such a rush to get home. My ex-wife and I live close to each other, so Noga can see either of us whenever she wants"

I listened, and I smiled. His voice sounded pleasant to me, and so did the things he was saying. It was too bad he'd gotten divorced, but the fact that he and his wife remained friends was a testament to the kind of person he was, and certainly to the kind of father he was. He showed me a photo from his wallet: a dark-skinned girl with smiling eyes and curly shoulder-length hair. When I looked at the picture, I couldn't help feeling a twinge of regret that I hadn't stayed with this man, that he wasn't the father of my children, that instead I had chosen Dan, who was cold and distant, who loved me as best he could, then got back to his own business. Whose love I hadn't felt for so many years that I was starting to wither.

And I thought about my kids, and promised myself not to let another night go by without hearing their voices. I would muster up all my courage, and call them. And if Dan wouldn't let me talk to them, I'd insist, and if they refused to hear my voice, I'd ask if I could at least hear theirs, even if everything they had to say was angry and defiant.

D'vir continued to tell me about his work and a new study he was involved in, but I was no longer listening. This unexpected encounter had taken me to all kinds of different places, places in which I was braver, smarter, and completely fearless. How had I turned into a shadow of myself?

Maybe it was the late hour or maybe I was just emotionally overwhelmed, but suddenly all I wanted to do was retreat to my little corner, pick up the phone, and dial the phone number which

I will always know by heart. After my children and husband had rejected me, I had been too scared to call. I had given up, and had been left without anything.

I apologized, and told D'vir I had to go. I asked him if I would see him again. "Same day, same time, same place," he said, smiling his winning smile, and again, I had to look away so my face wouldn't betray what was in my heart. This wasn't the right time for this; perhaps there would never be a right time. I left the café as quickly as I could, waved a distracted goodbye, and ran across the street, as though someone was chasing me.

I crossed Ha-Irya Street and Ibn-Gabirol Boulevard, turned left, then left again, until I reached my apartment. I hurried up the stairs, digging for my keys as I ran. I unlocked the door, slammed it shut behind me, and dashed over to the phone. I dialed and waited: no answer. I looked at the clock, and realized that in Seattle, it was almost noon: the kids were at school and Dan was at work. There was no way I could reach them. I collapsed on my bed and fell into a deep, dreamless sleep.

February 7, 1996

Hi Tamari,

It's the dawn of a new era, and it feels very strange. I'm so glad
you decided to open an e-mail account. Just think: you'll be able
to read my letters pretty much as soon as I write them! I won't
have to buy stamps, send the letters wait for you to read them,
and wait for you to respond. Instead, you can write back
immediately. It will be almost like having a live conversation. It
took me awhile to learn how to type; I suggest you start practicing
now. Something tells me this is the communication of the future,
and it won't be long before post offices become obsolete.
Correspondence will be quicker and more personal. A true
revolution.

Life here is the same as always: it's gray and rainy, the kids are in
school, Dan's working crazy hours. As usual, I'm keeping busy with
housekeeping, shopping, driving, cooking … those kinds of chores.
Thanks for the books, especially Yehudit Katzir's "Matisse has the
Sun in his Belly," which I couldn't put down. It reminded me a
little of us. It was about that era, back when we were young,
pretty girls... It all seems so far away, in both time and place. It
feels like a million years ago.

Yesterday I went to Snoqualmie Falls by myself. I brought a book
with me and stopped at a run-down inn for a cup of tea. For half
an hour, I was happy, and- for some reason- I missed you even
more than I do when I'm home. I'm counting the days until
Passover. It's just me and the kids. Dan can't join us, but I'm not

willing to give up Passover in Israel. I miss the warmth of the sun and the warmth of the people. My mother says that this year, we're going to celebrate at home. My brothers will come with their families, and we'll all be together. I'm glad. I think it's a wonderful idea, and I promised my mother I would help her with all the preparations.

Is there anything you need from the States? Another car seat? I've already bought presents for the kids, but if there's something you need, just e-mail me.

Love you and miss you,

Michal

P.S. Dan requests that you tell us in advance if you can't transfer the money on time. Call us, or send an e-mail. As I already told you, we'll be in serious trouble if we can't meet our payment deadlines for the loan we took out on your behalf.

φφφ

Like my father, my mother passed away unexpectedly, from a
massive heart attack. Her death left me shocked and heartbroken. My mother was, in essence, my whole family. My
brothers never made much of an effort to stay in touch, and the
distance between us- both physical and mental- made it that
much harder. When my mother died, I felt like I was all alone in
the world. I flew to Israel with Dan and the children. This time, he
understood that it wouldn't be right for him to leave me alone
with the kids, and for the first few days, he stood by me. Many
cousins and friends came to pay a *shiva* call, but Tamari wasn't
among them. I remember that she called me and offered all kinds
of excuses, but I was offended. I didn't tell her how hurt I was by
the way she treated me. After the *shiva,* I went to her house and
knocked on her door, but as usual, there was no answer. At the
end of that day- which was one of the longest days of my life- I
flew back to Seattle with Dan and the children. My life had
changed once again, and the loneliness I had felt before my
mother died became even worse. I felt abandoned, and the all-
consuming grief that I felt inside only intensified. I no longer
trusted Dan, and I didn't want to be near him. I was like a robot:
even though my children made me smile from time to time, I felt
nothing.

February 10, 1996

Tel Aviv

Hey Michalush,

Everything's fine- busy as usual. Doron is sick, and everything is falling on me. I am on the verge of falling apart. There's no difference between day and night, and of course there are all kinds of deadlines for work. Thank God the grandmothers can help us through this crazy time. I can't wait for your visit; I hope things calm down a little by then. I miss hanging out with you, just talking, without anyone bothering us. Do you think we can find a few peaceful hours?

If it's not too hard, yes, we do need a new carseat for Lianne, but only if it's not too hard. I know you'll be schlepping the kids and the suitcases, so if it doesn't work out, that's fine. Gotta run, Doron's calling for me.

Love,

Tamari

2005

I didn't call my children that night or the next, but for the first time in a long time, I woke up in the morning with renewed vigor. Instead of wanting to spend all day glued to the mattress, I wanted to go out into the world. I still had an uneasy feeling in the pit of my stomach, and I still missed my children so much it made my throat burn, but now I could see that perhaps, in spite of everything I wasn't completely alone in the world. For many years, I had thought that people only looked out for themselves; now I was going to give the people in my life a chance. Seeing D'vir made me want to get reacquainted with him, seeing Tamari helped me understand her weaknesses as well as mine, and seeing Ronit had given me hope that maybe, just maybe, all was not lost.

In the morning, the sun was shining, and I went outside to greet it. It didn't burn my skin, it caressed it, and I knew that it was time for me to find a job. Any job. That morning, I realized, I had neglected to check my neighbors' comings and goings, and it occurred to me that perhaps it wasn't my job to look after them. I couldn't understand how it had gotten to this point, but it didn't really matter. What mattered now was that I find a job. I sent out a pile of resumes, and then strolled around aimlessly, treating myself to ice cream and a walk to the beach After I got home, I decided to wait until the weekend to call the kids; it was only three more days. I tried to prepare myself for every possibility. I had an appointment with Ronit, the psychologist, and I knew that afterwards I would go to "The Bookworm" and wait for D'vir. He didn't have my phone number, and I didn't have his, but I knew that we would both end up in the same place. I hadn't spoken to

Tamari in a few days, though I did think of her often, and I decided that I didn't always have to be the one making the effort. If she wanted to, she knew where she could find me. I decided to give my conscience a break for once, to go with the flow, to try to make things better rather than focusing on what was missing.

In the next meetings, Ronit became less reticent and started asking more questions. She asked about my childhood and my family, and what family meant to me. I was taken aback by her last question, which went straight to my heart. Tears flowed from my eyes as I told her that for me, family meant unconditional love. I had seen it in my family when I was growing up, but I hadn't managed to attain it in my own life. My parents loved each other very much, despite the occasional screaming match. They showed their affection towards each other and towards us. I thought that the man I married would love me forever, but his love lost its way, and he became indifferent to my needs. Ronit wasn't shocked; when people get married, she said, they don't know what life has in store for them, and everyone has their own way of dealing with different situations. Sometimes a husband and wife grow together, and their love grows, too; sometimes it doesn't work out that way. But it's not a personal failure on my part or on Dan's. That's just how it is: life is unpredictable, and can take you in all different directions.

It's not like she said anything extraordinary or anything I hadn't already heard before, but this time her words took root, like seeds falling onto a ripe and ready field. Her simple words shook me to the core. I finally realized that for a long time, I had believed that I was a failure: as a person, a mother, a wife, a daughter, a sister, a friend. Although I knew that I was not the only one who had fallen short, the feeling of failure had penetrated my soul.

"And what about your kids?" Ronit asked.

"My kids are my world." I was swept away by a wave of shame at the thought of abandoning my children. "But I left them," I shot back.

"You didn't leave them," Ronit said. "You just took a little for yourself, you took a little break. It seems like you didn't have any other choice." I burst into tears once again, and she handed me a tissue. Was it possible that I wasn't a serial abandoner after all? It took a lot of courage for me to bring up this dark subject that was so shameful to me. What I needed most was to heal myself, to heal my relationship with my children, and now, all of a sudden, a sliver of doubt implanted itself within me: Was it possible that I was actually not the worst mother in the world? Was there any chance of reconciliation? I desperately wanted to fix things, I ached for my children, and I deeply regretted choosing myself over them.

Ronit tried to comfort me. "It's good that you took something for yourself, there's nothing wrong with taking, you're being too hard on yourself. Give happiness a chance. You deserve to be happy, just like everyone else in the world." I don't remember anything else she said. I left her office and walked over to "The Bookworm." I sat at the counter, and while I was waiting for D'vir, all I could think about was that maybe my relationship with my children could still be salvaged. Ronit was right: I hadn't really neglected them, I had just taken a little for myself, and if I hadn't done that, I would have gone mad.

Then D'vir came. He hugged me and kissed me on the cheek, and I leaned into his shoulder for a long time. When we sat down, he asked me if I had been crying. I said I had been, but it wasn't important. He looked at me and said that it was important to him. I couldn't bring myself to tell him about what happened in the therapist's office, so I just said, "I'm so glad you're here. Let's get some coffee. I'm not in the mood to talk about anything sad." He didn't pressure me. We ordered our coffee and sipped it in silence. I asked him how he was, and he told me about a lecture he had given at the university, and how much he loved sharing his thoughts and opening them for discussion. He enjoyed teaching, he said, even more than he enjoyed research, and if he had to give one of them up, he's not sure which one he'd choose.

I studied his face, trying to picture it without the wrinkles, and I could see the man he used to be. For a moment, I was twenty-something again, and I felt lighter than I'd felt in a long time, and all I wanted was to fall into his arms. After he told me about his day, I told him how I'd been looking for work, and I asked him how much time we had together before he had to go back to Haifa. He said he wasn't in a rush because his daughter was staying with her mother that night, and I suggested we go for a walk, since it was so lovely outside. We headed out towards Nordau Street, then continued on to the beach, walking side by side. We sat down on the sand and neither of us said a word, we just listened to the rippling of the waves, and I asked him if he could hug me, and he held me in his arms for a long time, and I breathed in the smell of his aftershave mingled with his sweat. I looked into his eyes, and I kissed him on the lips, then I smiled and looked into his eyes again. I said there was something I had to tell him, and he looked at me with serious eyes and waited quietly, and I told him, at great length, about all the years I had been a mother and a wife in far-off Seattle, and about Yonatan and Abigail. I could see the compassion in his eyes when I told him about my pain, and he didn't interrupt even once: not even during my occasional silences, not even when I choked on my words. I told him about how I'd abandoned my children, how I'd come back to Tel Aviv by myself, how I was living in my grandparents' apartment (after all, he knew them well and had visited them numerous times). Then I grew quiet. He asked me if I was OK, and I said, "Not really," and he pulled me into his arms, and I felt safe, and we just stayed like this, quietly for a long time. Then he told me he hoped it wasn't too late to repair the damage; then he corrected himself, and said, "I'm *sure* it's not too late to repair the damage." I said I hoped he was right. Then he said, "Do you know that you're a very special person?", and I asked him what he meant, and he said, "It takes tremendous courage to do what you did and to live with it every day," and a tear flowed onto my cheek, and he gently wiped it away with his big hand, and then we just listened to the waves, and all of a sudden, I felt at peace. I knew that I needed him more than I had needed anyone in a long time, and I wanted to rediscover this old, new person from head to toe, inside and out. I reached for his hand and kissed it, and I told him I was excited, and he said he was, too, and he felt like all the years that had passed were disappearing, and I didn't answer because I didn't want to think about anything, and he didn't talk, either, he just stood up and reached for me and pulled me close, and we stood there embracing, and I felt like I could drown inside him, and I told him I wanted him and he smiled and allowed me to lead him through the streets of Tel Aviv to my apartment and we made love, and for a little while I forgot about my pain and longing and was simply happy.

May 7, 1996

Seattle

Tamari,

How are things going? You haven't transferred any money in two months, and we're falling behind on our mortgage payments. Please tell me what's going on! Aside from that, I'm sorry I hardly got to see you. Whenever we go to Israel, it's a race against time, and you're always so busy, maybe next time.

Love,

Michal

May 10, 1996

Seattle

Tamari,

I hate to be a nag, but I couldn't get through by phone, and we need the money. Please get back to me.

Michal

May 14, 1996

Seattle

You finally got back to me, but you blew me off, and it wasn't pleasant. I don't understand why you had to be so nasty on the phone. We were only trying to help. Apparently, you couldn't care less.

Love you anyway,

Michal

2005

That was our last correspondence. I haven't written to her since then, nor has she written to me. Doron and Tamar never did pay us back, and I was deeply hurt by the coldness they showed us in return. I had lost my best friend, and I had to rethink everything I believed about the meaning of friendship. I retreated into myself. It wasn't only because of Tamari, but what happened between the two of us eroded my trust in all those closest to me. This happened at the same time that my relationship with Dan was in jeopardy, and I was counting on my friendship with Tamari to sustain me. But she didn't understand; she didn't see it. Perhaps she was so immersed in her own challenges, she wasn't capable of seeing. I don't know if that's what happened, and at this point it doesn't matter. If I had truly decided to give our friendship a chance, that meant forgiving her and finding space in my heart to love her. I had moved beyond my anger about the money- I had long resigned myself to the fact that we weren't going to get our money back- but this was happening at a time when my life was particularly difficult and empty. I wouldn't allow any new people into my world. I lived in a vacuum, at the edge of an abyss, and I was only just beginning to emerge. And now Tamari shows up.

That night, I slept the sleep of the just. I hadn't slept that well in years. When I finally woke up, D'vir wasn't in bed. I looked for him in the kitchen, and I found a note. He had caught the train to Haifa, he had meetings at the university, he didn't know my phone number but he was hoping I could call him that evening. The last sentence stressed me out a little: "I think I'm falling in love with you all over again...." But I smiled to myself, and tried to calm down, to open a window. I was giving so many things a chance; why shouldn't I give love a chance, too? Anyway, I was still married, even if it was just a formality. All these years I had been faithful to Dan. It had never even crossed my mind that there might be other men out there. I was committed to this partnership, for better or for worse. I don't know if he had any affairs while we were living together- I had never really thought about it. Marriage was sacred to me, and it still is, even now. It's just that the reality had changed, and I was seeing things differently. I had left, grieved, ached- I was still aching, mostly for my children- but for the first time I understood that I had the right to be happy, and if things weren't working out for me, it was my responsibility to change them. In those last few months, I had dared to venture out into the world without the armor that I had thought would protect me but ended up causing more harm than good.

Removing the armor allowed me to fully experience the night with D'vir, whose warm body enveloped me and whose words electrified both my heart and my mind. For a little while, I forgot who I was and where I had come from, and that hiatus revived me like a breath of life. I finally had the strength to become the person I really was.

But falling in love? I wasn't ready for that, and I certainly wasn't ready for the storm of emotions that went along with it. The load on my back was heavy enough. I took a long, cool shower and walked out into the Tel Aviv heat that I knew so well. I went to more offices, dropping off resumes and shaking hands; then I stopped at the local market to pick up a few things. I suddenly realized how long it had been since I had cooked myself a meal. It felt strange to prepare such small quantities of food, but I savored every bite. Afterwards I went back out and walked towards Ariella House, Tel Aviv's main library. It was already five in the evening, and the sun was beating down on my head. I stopped for a glass of lemonade, then walked on to the library. I climbed the stairs to the reading room and looked for a book that would be good for both my body and my soul. I knew I would contact my kids that weekend; I wasn't going to wait any longer. I would tell them that I loved them, and I would ask for their forgiveness. Maybe they'd listen. Maybe they'd be willing to forgive me.

When I got home, I called D'vir. He was happy to hear from me, and said he hoped his note from that morning hadn't shaken me up too much. I admitted that it had shocked me a bit, and I asked him to give me time. He had all the time in the world, he said. He wasn't rushing off anywhere. I told him I didn't know if I could commit to anything right now. There were so many obstacles lying ahead, and it wasn't simple. We agreed to meet at "The Bookworm" the following week; until then, we could talk on the phone. I gave him my number, glad that he wasn't pushing me in one direction or another.

After I hung up with D'vir, I called Tamari and invited her and her kids to Friday night dinner. She was surprised and touched, and said that nothing would please her more. Relieved, I went to bed, filled with both a new kind of peace and giddy anticipation.

At precisely seven, Tamari knocked on the door. I couldn't wait to see her kids, who had grown so much; I'd never even met the youngest one. Lianni had blossomed into a beautiful young woman; she looked like both Doron and Tamari. Tomer, almost a Bar Mitzvah, was quiet and cheerful, and the little girl was sweet and bouncy and bursting with joy. They filled my apartment with a fresh, breezy energy, and the evening was delightful. We didn't get into any serious conversations. I assumed Tamari had prepared her children for Yonatan and Abigail's absence; they didn't ask any questions. The meal was a painful reminder of how much I missed my own children. My only comfort was knowing that I was going to call them the next day, with the hope that it wasn't too late. As we were clearing the table, Tamari thanked me for the meal, and invited me to join them at the beach the next day. I appreciated the offer, but I explained that I had already made plans, that I would be having a difficult conversation with Dan and the kids. She offered to come over and give me moral support; I thanked her and told her how much that offer meant to me, but this was something I had to do by myself.

I walked the four of them to the door and waved goodbye. None of my neighbors were outside. I went back in, closing the door behind me, and listened to the silence all around me. This silence accompanies me everywhere, every day and every night. On the hottest days, when I turn on the air conditioner and close the windows, the quiet is almost overwhelming. Now, I turned off the a/c and opened the windows as far as they would go. The noise of the city floated into my bedroom and brought it to life. I had returned to the world.

φφφ

The phone rang and rang, and I waited patiently. I wasn't going to give up. Finally, I heard my son's voice from the other end of the world. He recognized my voice immediately.

"Mom?" he shouted. Hearing the word "Mom" brought back all kinds of feelings that I had thought were gone forever. My eyes filled with tears.

"Yes, it's me," I said. "Yonatan. I love you, my child."

"I love you, too, Mom." He said the word again, shattering me into a thousand pieces.

There was silence. When I spoke again, I choked on my words and practically shouted. "I'm sorry, my son, I'm sorry."

"Mom, are you coming home? When are you coming home? We miss you so much."

"Yonatan," I said, "I'm not sure. But I want you to know that I love you, and that I'm sorry."

"Where are you anyway?" I was flabbergasted. Surely Dan had told them what was going on. The thought that Dan might not tell them where I was had never even crossed my mind. Shock and anger pulsed through me, and I could hardly breathe. Why on earth would he want them to worry so much? Because he couldn't cope with their questions? Dan was still Dan, distant and aloof even with his own children, hurtful and incomprehensible.

"I'm in Tel Aviv, in my grandparents' apartment," I said softly. I didn't want my son to sense even a trace of the anger and frustration that were churning inside me. His voice was the most beautiful sound I'd ever heard, and I wanted the moment to last. "Where did you think I was?"

"I didn't know what to think, Mom. Dad just said that you left and there was no way go get in touch with you. He said you abandoned us, and you didn't want to have any contact with us anymore. Is that true? And he refuses to talk about you. Abigail and I didn't know what to think. Did you really not want to have anything to do with us?"

It had never occurred to me that not only would Dan not reassure them, he would actually turn them against me. Again, I felt betrayed, desperate, and furious: what did he worry them for? Why didn't he tell them the truth? Less than five minutes into our conversation, I heard Abigail shouting at her brother. "You're talking to Mom! Give me the phone!" He protested, but he gave it to her. As soon as she started talking, both of us burst into tears. No matter how hard I tried to play the part of the mature adult, I couldn't control myself. We talked and we cried. Abigail pleaded with me to come back home, and I told her I couldn't. "You can't? Or you don't want to?" I could hear Yonatan's voice in the background. "I can't," I said. "Come visit me. It's almost school vacation."

"I think you'd better talk to Dad about this," Yonatan said. "Personally, I'm totally fine with that. The day school ends, I'm on the plane." Abigail echoed his sentiments, and suddenly I was in heaven. I was so grateful to them; until that moment I felt like I didn't deserve their love. Until the day I left, it had been them and me, together. They hadn't forgotten how much I love them.

Still, I had to clear it with Dan. He wasn't home, and I promised the kids I would talk to him. They asked me if they should tell him they talked to me, and I said yes. No more secrets. From now on, everything would be out in the open.

Our conversation continued for a long time; nobody wanted to hang up. I wanted to hear as much as I could, and I was heard by them, too, even if only briefly. I told them, over and over again, that I was sorry, that I loved them and I always would. As we wrapped up our conversation, I repeated my promise that I would talk to Dan. I wasn't going to let him wipe me out of my children's lives. I'm not a mother who abandons her children; I'm a mother who was struggling, and my husband, instead of sharing my pain, banished me from his life and from the lives of my children.

After I hung up, I made myself a big glass of iced coffee and carried it over to the window, trying to calm the storm of emotions that had taken hold of me. I wanted to embrace my children, to hold them close to my heart. I couldn't wait any longer. What if Dan wouldn't allow them to visit?

It was early on Saturday morning. The front yard was quiet, and there were barely any cars on the street. Saturday morning in the beginning of Israel's endless summer.... Nobody can grasp how much I had missed the heat. Everyone's always complaining about the *hamsins*- the heatwaves- and the mugginess and the never-ending heat, but I can't get enough of the heat and the humidity, or of being surrounded by Hebrew. After so many years of feeling like I didn't belong, here I finally felt like I had come home. It was a wonderful feeling.

When I called the following day, Dan answered the phone. He sounded cold and stoical, and he asked me if I had changed my plans. I said that I was staying here for now, but I wanted the children to come visit me. I offered to send them the tickets. I didn't have the money to do that yet, but I was hoping with all my heart to get a job soon. It was stressful, but I had faith that I would succeed. Dan said he had to think about it, and talk it over with the kids. We decided I'd call him again in a few days. He didn't say anything about the two of us, and I was relieved. For my part, I didn't mention the fact that he had kept so much from my kids. And what else was there to say? I didn't love him anymore, and I'd had enough of the estranged partnership we'd had for so many years. More than anything else, I wanted him to let the children visit me, and I didn't want to get into any arguments that might jeopardize that possibility. As we spoke, I sensed that both of us were ready to move on, move beyond our irreconcilable differences, to continue on our own separate paths. I didn't know what would happen with D'vir, but I felt like I was more open than ever to the kind of partnership that was first and foremost a close and loving friendship. Dan was no longer my friend. Maybe D'vir could be.

I got ready to go to the beach. I put on a bathing suit that I had recently bought, and my grandmother's straw hat. I slipped on the water shoes I use every summer without fail, and I began the short walk to my beloved beach, to enjoy the day with Tamari and her children.

Tel-Aviv Seattle 2014

CPSIA information can be obtained at www.ICGtesting.com
Printed in the USA
LVOW04s1249181214

419406LV00005B/468/P